PENGUIN BOOKS

EVERYBODY'S DOING IT

Andrea Warren is a journalist with fifteen years' experience writing for the popular and medical press. She presents seminars on writing and communications skills for corporations and medical groups. She is a former newspaper reporter, trade magazine editor, and high school English teacher, with master's degrees in both English and journalism. She is the author of four books; her latest is *Recovering from Breast Cancer*.

Jay Wiedenkeller is director of the child development center at Saint Joseph Health Center in Kansas City. A specialist in early childhood education, he is a popular workshop presenter for parenting groups. He completed his graduate studies at the University of Kansas, supplementing undergraduate work in psychology. A second-degree black belt in Tae Kwondo, he teaches the martial arts in the Kansas City area.

Married since 1981, Ms. Warren and Mr. Wiedenkeller share the parenting of two teenage daughters, one each from former marriages.

EVERYBODY'S DOING IT

How to Survive
Your Teenagers' Sex Life
(and Help Them Survive It, Too)

ANDREA WARREN
& JAY WIEDENKELLER

PENGUIN BOOKS

PENGUIN BOOKS
Published by the Penguin Group
Penguin Books USA Inc., 375 Hudson Street,
New York, New York 10014, U.S.A.
Penguin Books Ltd, 27 Wrights Lane,
London W8 5TZ, England
Penguin Books Australia Ltd, Ringwood,
Victoria, Australia
Penguin Books Canada Ltd, 10 Alcorn Avenue,
Toronto, Ontario, Canada M4V 3B2
Penguin Books (N.Z.) Ltd, 182–190 Wairau Road,
Auckland 10, New Zealand

Penguin Books Ltd, Registered Offices:
Harmondsworth, Middlesex, England

First published in Penguin Books 1993

10 9 8 7 6 5 4 3 2 1

A NOTE TO THE READER
The ideas, procedures, and suggestions contained in this book are not intended as a substitute for consulting with your physician. All matters regarding one's health require medical supervision.

LIBRARY OF CONGRESS CATALOGING-IN-PUBLICATION DATA
Warren, Andrea.
Everybody's doing it : how to survive your teenagers' sex life and help them survive it too / Andrea Warren and Jay Wiedenkeller.
p.   cm.
Includes bibliographical references.
ISBN 0 14 017151 7
1. Sex instruction for teenagers—United States.   2. Teenagers—United States—Sexual behavior.   3. Parent and teenager—United States.   4. Sexual ethics for teenagers.   I. Wiedenkeller, Jay.   II. Title.
HQ57.W25   1993
307.7'0835—dc20

Printed in the United States of America
Set in Electra
Designed by Brian Mulligan

For our mothers,
our daughters,
and Derek, with love
and for Ben, always

A WORD TO
OUR READERS

When we began writing this book, we decided that if it was going to
be relevant, readers needed to hear actual voices. Accomplishing this
has involved endless hours of tape transcription, but we feel we have
succeeded in conveying the reality and immediacy that were our goal.

Many people spoke to us both on and off the record as we put all
of this together. We used actual names when we give both a first and
last name. We changed names when we use only a first name, and
in some instances we changed identifying information to protect the
person's identity.

We are grateful to all the teenagers and adults who so generously
assisted us. You know who you are. You have helped to give this
book its authenticity and honesty.

A.W.

J.W.

CONTENTS

INTRODUCTION

If you are a concerned parent who knows or suspects that your teen is sexually active or soon may be, we invite you to take a journey with us.

We parents know that ours is a perilous world for anybody who's sexually active and not in a long-term monogamous relationship. The world is particularly perilous for young people who may be emotionally vulnerable and not properly protected against pregnancy, disease, and exploitation.

The teen years are difficult under any circumstances. Young people are busy creating their own identities, and this process involves separating from us and exerting their independence. This is a normal developmental process for teens, but it can create power struggles and tension in the parent-child relationship if there are differing views and little or no effective communication between parents and their teenagers.

The issue of sex and teenagers can be particularly troublesome. The list of problems associated with indiscriminate, early, and/or unprotected sex includes emotional and physical risks, unplanned pregnancies, AIDS and other STDs, and sexual violence.

In our quest to help our teenagers avoid such problems, we may run smack up against the "it won't happen to me" mentality so characteristic of teenagers. As adults we *know* that bad things *do* happen to good people, that the more risks you take, the greater the chances of disaster. Most of us have made mistakes ourselves that we would like to keep our children from repeating.

Sex is an emotional topic that many of us are not comfortable discussing. Views differ, even between caring parents or within extended families who are raising teenagers. Some of us strongly believe that sex outside of marriage is wrong under any circumstances. Others, that sex is not a topic parents and children should talk about, *period*. Some of us don't care what our teenagers do or when, as long as they are taking care of themselves. Some of us hope our teenagers will wait until they are in their late teens or twenties before they become sexually active. Some of us don't know *what* we believe about teens and sex because we received such mixed signals about sex when we were growing up. A few of us try not to think about it at all, because we've told our kids not to do it and we want to believe they always do what we say.

Whatever we believe, in today's sexually difficult climate we know that we can't be indifferent to the topic of sex if we are raising teenagers. Nor can we rely on schools and community organizations to equip our children with the knowledge they need to protect themselves in the event they are sexually active. While many sex-education courses do a fairly good job of teaching facts, few of them tackle the tough subjects of sexual consequences, values, building relationships, intimacy and pleasure, and sexual orientation. These must be our responsibility.

One particularly difficult dilemma facing parents is giving teens the knowledge they need to protect themselves both emotionally and physically when we don't approve of their being sexually active—whether they already are or we suspect they may eventually be. Along with this, some parents fear that giving teens such information delivers the message that they are being given a green light to have sex.

The mixed feelings and guilt many of us have about sex and our own sexuality make all these issues even more troublesome.

As the parents of teenagers, the two of us identify with all these situations and feelings. When sex became an issue in our household, we set out to learn why so many teenagers have become sexually active, with what results, and why this is so difficult a topic for our generation.

Before we begin our journey, let's take a glimpse backward to see how the sexual values of our generation were formed and what we have passed along to our children.

We who are parents of teenagers in the nineties carry around a lot of baggage about sex. Our values about our own sexuality were being formed in the 1950s, when society touted virginity before marriage as a goal, particularly for females (unlike today, when virginity often weighs heavily upon both sexes).

The movies we grew up with were full of sex, but it took place behind closed doors and almost always between married couples. Words like *masturbation*, *orgasm*, *homosexuality*, and *condom* were not part of everyday conversation. For too many of us, our sex education consisted of embarrassed mothers giving a brief explanation of menstruation to daughters, and stern fathers warning sons to "keep it in your pants."

We were raised to be modest, virtuous, polite, and thrifty. Of course we were interested in sex—that's universal to both males and females and always has been—but it wasn't fodder for television talk shows and the rest of the media. Teenage girls didn't wear thong bikinis and rhinestone bullet bras. Condom machines were not located in the rest rooms in high schools. Unwed motherhood was not commonplace. And even if their marriages were miserable, parents stayed together.

Sex was a source of guilt for most of us. It was treated by our parents and by society as secret, sordid, and dirty. We were not supposed to be interested in it, so we pretended we weren't, even though we all were. We didn't have access to information about it and were not allowed to ask our parents the frank questions we wanted answers to, so most of us were fairly uninformed about it. We certainly weren't being told that we were all sexual beings and that our interest in sex and sexuality was normal, natural, and healthy.

Quite the opposite. In the eyes of some religions, particularly the Catholic religion, a woman was a "vessel of sin." Sex and procreation were Adam and Eve's—and hence humankind's—punishment for the fall from grace. Girls were instructed to be worthy of wearing white on their wedding days and were taught that men didn't want "damaged goods" for wives. To "go all the way," as we called it, instantly branded a girl as "loose" or "fast." You were a good girl or a bad girl, and there were no shades of gray in between. Guys could get away with more, but they usually didn't. It was, to put it mildly, a sexually repressive time.

And then came the so-called sexual revolution of the sixties, ushered in by the introduction of the birth-control pill. For many of us just coming into young adulthood, it was a heady time of free love. We were the "Love Generation," raised in the affluence of the post–World War II boom economy by parents who had grown up in the tough times of the Depression and made up for the deprivation they suffered by spoiling us.

Like every generation, we rebelled against our parents. But because we were so spoiled and life had been so easy for us, we did it with noisy abandon—and our rebellious phase happened to coincide with the sexual revolution.

We tormented and scandalized our parents and grandparents with our bell-bottoms, beads, long hair, incense, drugs, communes, and rock 'n' roll. Freed from the tyranny of pregnancy by the pill and with penicillin available to cure any nasty diseases that might be lurking about, we suppressed the sexual guilt we had been raised with and began to act as though we had invented sex. Some of us took off our clothes at rock concerts, embraced movies full of nudity, cohabited, and produced an occasional love child named Starshine or Moonbeam.

Others of us lived more traditional, monogamous lives but still reveled in the spirit of the sixties. We forsook our parents' materialism and the perfectly-cared-for house in the suburbs to join the Peace Corps, teach school in Appalachia, heat our modest little houses with wood-burning stoves, work actively for civil rights, wear peace symbols around our necks, and sing "Give Peace a Chance." We studied yoga and learned to play the guitar. We went to love-ins and teach-ins, read poetry, majored in American Studies, and endlessly argued politics.

Whatever route we chose, for all of us the free lunch came to an end in the mid-seventies.

Our grandfathers fought the Kaiser and our fathers fought Hitler and Mussolini to make the world safe for us. And then we lost our war in Vietnam, a country no bigger than the state of Kansas, against a poorly equipped army of hungry peasants.

When we looked around at the Great Society we had helped create, we saw the My Lai massacre in Vietnam, Kent State, Watergate, and the Pentagon Papers. We saw our brothers and friends returning from the war injured, bitter, and drug-dependent.

Disillusioned, feeling guilt about the war and guilt about our decadent lifestyles, we began to look inward. Our soul searching led us to a desire for a new code of honesty. Fallout included the dissolution of many marriages. The divorce rate soared, doubling between 1965 and 1975, peaking in 1979 at 5.3 divorces a year per 1,000 people—the highest in history. We gave up pot and started to jog and to think about receding hairlines. We read Alex Haley's *Roots*. We hung out in singles bars for a while, then, tired of bed hopping, we got married again, bought houses, and settled down, many of us to become parents for the first time.

We had lived through unsettling times. Now we had a clear focus: to raise our children without all the hangups, the hypocrisy, and the guilt we grew up with. We were determined, just as every generation before us was, to give our children what we had missed.

Our parents raised us with material wealth but denied us intimate access to themselves. We couldn't talk to them about feelings. When it came to our sexuality, we had to live secretly from them. We were going to make darn sure our kids could talk to us about anything. They would think for themselves, make their own choices, be whatever they wanted to be. "Free to be you and me" and "I am Sam, Sam I am."

We wanted family life to be wholesome and natural. No cardboard suburbs for *our* kids. Many of us lived in the country, put solar panels on our houses, and drove conservative little foreign cars that didn't burn much gas. We opened cooperative preschools and cooperative groceries. We watched *Sesame Street* with our children and planted gardens with them and fed them organic sprouts and tofu. We taught them to be blind to the color of people's skins. Our mothers had given us bottles and fed us according to predetermined schedules. We breast-fed our babies whenever they were hungry. We gave our sons dolls and put overalls on our daughters and told them both they could grow up to be airline pilots, scientists, or president, taking special pride in our assertive, independent daughters.

But the times changed again, and our simple lifestyles went by the wayside in the eighties. We turned into yuppies with Cuisinarts and espresso machines. We quit teaching school and went to law school. We exchanged degrees in social work for degrees in business administration.

We took all that energy our generation was famous for and put it into our careers. Some of us entered third or even fourth marriages. We dressed our free-thinking, guilt-free children in designer jeans and leather jackets and Nike Air sneakers and bought them Commodore computers and video games, alarming even our own materialistic-minded parents with all the ways we found to indulge and spoil their grandchildren.

Unlike our parents' generation, when moms could stay home to raise their children, our generation needed two incomes to support this lifestyle. Because of the ravages of divorce, many dads were also paying child support to first families. More and more young families were a hodgepodge of "yours, mine, and ours," and few of us knew how to navigate the turbulent waters of stepfamilyhood successfully. We didn't have our extended families to help us the way our parents and grandparents had. Mom and Dad had moved to Sun City. Our fractured families were scattered everywhere, leaving us isolated.

Many of us were either single parents or caught up in demanding careers. Because we wanted the best for our children, we often had them and us overscheduled, leaving little time for more than superficial communication. And while we paid lip service to their free spirits and told them they could come to us with any problem, we weren't really any better at communication than our parents had been. So many of us were silently imposing the same values we had grown up with: You can't talk to me about sex. You shouldn't be thinking about sex. You certainly shouldn't be *having* sex. If you go against what I believe, I will think less of you.

All this confusion has given rise to uncertainty and stress. The

American family is undergoing dramatic change. Everyone's tired; kids don't get enough attention. We're under financial pressure and uncertain about the future. Violence is commonplace. Gangs rule many city streets. Suicide is the number-two cause of death among teenagers (accidents are first). Their use of drugs and alcohol is at epidemic proportions. They are becoming sexually active at younger and younger ages, taking for granted the sexual revolution we experienced but without the guilt that had strangled us. The problems of AIDS and other sexually transmitted diseases (STDs), abortions, and babies born out of wedlock are costly in terms of both human misery and the strain on our country's financial and medical resources.

Our message to our children was that they could have it all and they could have it now. What we have produced is a generation of children who don't wait for anything and don't just say no to anything.

Even if our values have been passed along, our children are tempted at every turn by the media. They love television, the electronic babysitter, and they consider sitcom characters part of the family. Our children turn it on and there's Murphy Brown, a single mom; Doogie Howser, M.D., and his lost virginity; teen heartthrob Brenda on *Beverly Hills 90210* going through a pregnancy scare; the teenage daughter on *Married: With Children* behaving, in her sex-starved mother's words, like a slut; Roseanne putting her nonvirgin daughter on the pill. On the daytime soaps, every other scene seems to take place in bed.

Our children see Wilt Chamberlain, interviewed on the publication of his autobiography, talking about sleeping with 20,000 different women. "The world revolves around sex," he says, and who could argue after listening to him? They hear Magic Johnson, who says he slept with only a thousand women, more or less, revealing that he is HIV-positive, and Woody Allen justifying his sexual relationship with Mia Farrow's daughter.

They watch Anita Hill accusing then–Supreme Court nominee

Clarence Thomas of sexual harassment, William Kennedy Smith charged with date rape, Mike Tyson found guilty of rape, and naval officers accused of sexual assault in the Tailhook scandal.

They see talk-show hosts serve up a daily fare of people born of incestuous relationships, teenage prostitutes, women seduced by priests, men who pretend to be women while giving phone sex to men, women married to men young enough to be their sons, men who commit bigamy, women who fall in love with their fathers-in-law, stepfathers who fall in love with their stepdaughters, stepbrothers and stepsisters who have affairs with each other—you name it: if it has to do with sex, it's fodder for daytime television.

They're exposed to ads for Camel cigarettes featuring dromedaries whose faces strongly resemble male genitalia, in spite of the company's denial of any similarity. They hear songs on the teen hit parade with titles like "I Want Your Sex" and "I Want to Sex You Up."

They see Hollywood dish up flesh in practically every film, including scenes in PG-13 movies that would make our grandparents blush. They need a score card to keep up with the stars who live together and/or have children together, while the ever-vigilant media make sure they know who Cher's and Madonna's young flavor-of-the-month boyfriends are.

They keep up with the sex lives of British royalty and American politicians, who, as always, are fair game for the sex-and-weirdo tabloids displayed in supermarkets—supermarkets that now carry big displays of condoms right next to all the feminine hygiene products advertised on television.

With an estimated 70 percent of graduating high school seniors now sexually active, with AIDS doubling every year in the under-twenty population, with one in seven teenagers infected with another of the many sexually transmitted diseases, and with one in four babies being born to unwed teenage mothers, how do we respond as a society? How do we respond as concerned parents?

When one of our teenage daughters became sexually active, we wanted to understand why she would defy the values she had been raised with. In our search for insight we visited with teenagers, young adults, parents, physicians, nurse practitioners, psychologists, school counselors, and teachers. We heard wise things and stupid things. We had our values and attitudes challenged. Sometimes we challenged others'.

All of these conversations were lively, sometimes heated, sometimes painful, and always insightful. We found that with the exception of teenagers themselves, everyone, whether liberal or conservative, religious or not, is concerned with how quickly children grow up today, beginning formerly adults-only behaviors at younger and younger ages while facing greater risks than ever before.

We learned many things about teens, parents, and the forces that bring them together or tear them apart. We learned that parents cannot decide if and when their teenagers will choose to be sexually active. We discovered a greater appreciation and understanding of sex and sexuality and their roles in all people's lives, whether heterosexual or homosexual. We also gained insight into the teenage psyche; knowledge about the medical community and its approach to sexually active teens; an understanding of homosexuality and its effects on families; an appreciation of the choices facing pregnant teens and their consequences for families; and information about how to communicate with teenagers successfully and help them to be physically and emotionally healthy if they decide to be sexually active.

As you journey along with us, we think that at the very least you will, like us, gain some insight into yourself, our society, and the world of teens. You will also come away with a more effective way of interacting with your teenagers about sex and sexuality so that you can have a sense of peace about this difficult issue.

Let's begin.

EVERYBODY'S
DOING
IT

CHAPTER 1

NICE PARENTS TURN INTO SEX POLICE!

We never thought that parenting two teenage daughters would be a piece of cake, but until midway through their sixteenth year it went well.

Marissa and Alexandra aren't twins, but their birthdays are only a few months apart. Ours is a blended family. When we married in 1981, we each had full custody of a seven-year-old daughter. For a long time the girls were best friends and did everything together. About the time they turned eleven they began to distance themselves from each other, playing together when other kids from the neighborhood were included but also starting to have their own friends and their own interests.

Peaceful coexistence disappeared midway through their thirteenth year. Impassioned disagreements arose. Sharing possessions turned into unauthorized "borrowing" from each other. They accused each other of unfair treatment, of not taking correct phone messages, of saying untrue things behind the other's back, and of not cleaning up their shared bathroom. If there was room for conflict over anything, they found it.

We pursued our longtime policy of refusing to get involved as long as problems were not serious. Work it out, we told them. Try to see your sister's point of view. No physical contact allowed. Reason with each other.

Though our noninvolvement often frustrated them more than whatever they were mad at each other about, for the most part it worked. We were not constantly trying to settle arguments, and they learned the art of compromise.

We used a different approach when it came to their sex education. We had both grown up in homes where sex and sexuality were never discussed. Like so many of our peers who are now fortysomething like us and who were teenagers in the sixties, we found that our inability to communicate with our own parents about sex, and the confusion and guilt we brought to adulthood about sex had made us determined that it would be different for our children. We wanted them to understand their bodies and to feel comfortable with their sexuality. We wanted them to like being female. We read to them— books like *Where Did I Come From?* that explained about sperm and eggs and how they got together—and we talked to them about the changes taking place inside them as they got older. When they started their periods, we expressed our happiness for them that they were growing up.

To further ease their transition into their maturing bodies, we enrolled them in a highly recommended year-long course in sex education, entrusting the physician instructor to teach them everything they needed to know that their school health classes might not cover.

As far as we were concerned, we had all bases covered. They saw us in a happy marriage with open communication. We assured them we were willing to talk with them about anything and urged them to come to us with their concerns. If the topic of sex came up, they would act embarrassed, blush fiercely, and then make jokes or terminate the conversation as rapidly as possible, but that didn't deter us. That we could talk with them at all seemed by comparison with our own silent upbringings to be an achievement.

While we were flexible and liberal in most things, we were also cautious. We insisted that their makeup and clothing be in good taste (even when their friends' weren't) and that their behavior around their friends of both sexes be appropriate (even when their friends' behaviors were questionable).

These policies didn't always make us popular, but aside from occasional conflicts between the girls, we felt satisfied—and maybe even a bit smug—because everything seemed to be fine. We were comfortable with parenthood and appreciated our daughters' individuality—and they were definitely different from each other.

Marissa was rather shy, artistic, and introspective. She liked to do things with only one or two friends at a time and would spend endless hours in her room, experimenting with hairstyles, talking with friends on the phone, and doing her homework. She kept her room neat and orderly and paid careful attention to how she dressed.

Alex was outgoing, experimental, and self-confident. She liked to have a gang around her. When she was home, she usually had at least one friend with her. Though a good student, she kept everything she owned in a state of upheaval and would dive into her clothes and rush off to school at the last possible moment each morning.

When the girls were approaching the middle of their sixteenth year, it was Alex who metamorphosed into the Teenager from Hell.

She began to fight with us about her curfew, her friends, her chores, her room, how much she used her telephone, what she ate, and what she wore. Black became her favorite color, and many a day she was dressed in black from head to foot. To our chagrin, she started to smoke. The expression on her face became a perpetual scowl. She was sulky and secretive, always wanting to have a later curfew, to borrow the car, to be out with friends. She got into the routine of staying awake until she dropped, her stereo going, talking on the phone until many a night we had to take it away from her.

Formerly pleasant family meals now invariably ended in conflict. She regularly accused us of being too strict, too old, and too out of it. Everything seemed to boil down to issues of freedom and values—hers versus ours. She could not understand why we thought we had anything to complain about.

In the face of this onslaught, we strove hard to remain reasonable, with no yelling, no retaliating, and no taking personally what she was doing to us. We tried to confront and respond to each issue. When she broke the rules or was rude to us, she lost a privilege or on rare occasions was grounded. We were convinced that the storm would gradually pass as this strong-willed child matured, provided we could just hold our own.

Sometimes our resolve worked. When we found out she had skipped school several times, we asked school officials to throw the book at her and give her their maximum punishment in addition to the grounding she received from us. They did—three Saturday in-school suspensions. She wasn't caught skipping out again.

But all this was only prelude to what happened when she began to date the Boyfriend.

Like her, he was in full rebellion against adults, but his rebellion approached the illegal. He had a dark side that was scary. He was a kid with some major problems, including drugs, and we were alarmed about how he might influence her. We voiced our concerns but might as well have talked to the wall. She thought that he was wonderful and that she was the only one in the world who understood him.

As we always had with our daughters' friends, we welcomed him into our home, determined to try to respect her choice. In spite of our uneasiness, for the first few weeks things seemed to go well. Then on an early spring day we spotted them cozied together in the backyard hammock. There was something troublesome about it. It was the suggestion of sex.

Ridiculous, we assured each other. Both of our daughters were aware of our views concerning sex. Without talking about morality and religion, we had told them that sex was for when one was "older" and in a "committed" relationship. We didn't define "older" and "committed," but we knew they knew what we meant.

Just to be on the safe side, we decided to remind Alex that guys can sometimes put a lot of pressure on girls to have sex and that if this happened to her, she should say no, and say it firmly.

So that evening, as we did when we had matters of real importance to discuss, we requested that she sit down with us at the kitchen table to talk. She was leery, but she sat. We delivered our message, our voices full of motherly and fatherly concern. "If you feel that he's pressuring you, you might try telling him you don't like it, and be sure the tone of your voice makes this clear to him," we suggested.

We smiled encouragingly at her.

Alex just sat there, her body stone. She stared at the wall, the defiant look on her face saying as loudly as words that we had stumbled into private territory where we were *not* welcome.

"I can take care of myself," she said sullenly, refusing to look at us, though surely she felt our hurt and surprise.

"We just thought—"

She jumped up. "Can I go now? I have homework to do."

The truth was rapidly dawning on both of us. We looked at each other and then at her. "Do you . . . are you and he . . ." one of us began.

"Yes!" she blurted, jumping up from her chair. "Now can I go?"

"Protection!" one of us managed to say as she bolted toward the door. "Are you using protection?"

For a moment she hesitated. "We *know* what we're doing. We're not *stupid*."

"We'll take you to see a doctor. We'll make an appointment immediately—"

"What*ever*," she said, dashing out. "Can't talk anymore. Homework."

We stared blankly at each other. The truth was obvious: She was having sex. Very possibly *unprotected* sex. How could this be? And how could we have been so naive? Only a year before she had been a good kid, going out with groups of friends, having fun, enjoying her adolescence and allowing us to enjoy it too. Then the problems started—the smoking, the arguments, the adolescent angst. And now . . .

We spent a sleepless night, each of us wrestling with our thoughts. In becoming sexually active, Alex was participating in an activity we felt was reserved for responsible adults. She *wasn't* an adult! She *didn't* belong in that world—and *we didn't want her there!* Also, at age sixteen she lacked the necessary maturity to assure that her sexual experience was emotionally healthy. She could get hurt. Then there were the mind-boggling risks: pregnancy and the sexually transmitted diseases, including, God forbid, AIDS. We knew nothing of the Boyfriend's sexual history, but we knew he'd had many girlfriends. That meant that if he *had* been having sex, Alex was sleeping with every girl *he'd* slept with.

When morning finally came, we tried to console each other. At least she'll let us help her, we said. At least she's not pregnant. We looked at each other. Is she?

Later, comparing emotions, we discovered that both of us reacted to our daughter's revelation with surprise, disappointment, anger, worry, and sadness.

Surprise that she hadn't come to us to say she was thinking of having sex with her boyfriend and wanted our help in getting protection (though we must admit it would have been hard for her to do this, since she knew we would disapprove).

Disappointment that she would go against what we had taught her, vague though our message might have been as to what we felt was an appropriate age for sex. She had to know that we thought sixteen was too young.

Anger that she would risk pregnancy and disease—anger not only for her sake but for ours as well.

Worry that pregnancy and/or disease might already be realities.

The *sadness* was harder to define. It had to do with a loss of innocence and an end to childhood. This emotion turned out to be tougher for us to come to grips with than any of the others.

Our first phone call the next morning was to our pediatrician for a referral to a gynecologist. If Alex was having sex, then we wanted her in the hands of a physician who would help her stay healthy and disease-free. When we explained to our pediatrician what was going on, our feelings overwhelmed us. How could our child do this to us? She was too *young!* This was *absolutely unacceptable.*

Our pediatrician strongly agreed, delivering a diatribe about the irresponsibility of today's teenagers. She recommended we get Alex on the pill before she became a child with a child, and gave us a rundown of all the nasty diseases lurking around. Did the Boyfriend use condoms? Did we know how many sex partners he'd already had? Did we know that most boys refuse to use condoms, and of those who do, most use them incorrectly?

With panic starting to edge out our anger, we contacted the recommended gynecologist, pleading for a quick appointment. We were in luck: the sympathetic receptionist had just received a cancellation for the following afternoon.

The next morning we called the gynecologist on the speaker-phone so we could both talk. "We're very upset about this," we told her, our words tumbling out. "We don't know how you feel about teenage girls and sex, but please don't convey the message to our daughter that what she's doing is okay and that just because we're putting her on the pill she's got a green light on her sex life."

The gynecologist told us she was straightforward with her teenage patients and made no moral judgments.

"However, I must forewarn you," she said, "that sometimes parents get very angry with me because I must observe patient confidentiality. I can't share any medical information with you about your daughter without her permission."

It took a minute for this to sink in. "You mean, if she's pregnant, you won't be able to tell us unless she says it's okay?" we finally asked.

"Exactly."

For the second time in twenty-four hours, we were stunned. The law and the medical community were severing our rights to be involved in life-altering decisions for our daughter. She was *only sixteen! Something was terribly wrong!*

That afternoon we picked up Alex at her suburban Kansas City high school and drove in silence to the gynecologist's office. Though she seemed calm, probably, like us, she had knots in her stomach. She didn't ask why we had both taken time off work to come with her. She knew: Our joint presence indicated how concerned we were. She didn't challenge us.

When the three of us were ushered into the doctor's private office, we bumbled through a conversation about types of birth control, safe sex, and the necessity of condoms. Alex acted incredibly cool the entire time.

Out in the waiting room while she had her first gynecological exam, we talked in hushed tones about what we would do if she were pregnant—assuming she even chose to share such information with us. No answers came to us. Our systems were already on overload. Nothing was making any sense.

And then Alex and the doctor came into the waiting room and the doctor handed us the prescription for birth-control pills.

"She won't need to start them for a few days because today is the first day of her period," the doctor said, looking us in the eyes. We silently blessed her for letting us know in a legally permissible way that there was no pregnancy to contend with.

Though our moods were much lighter than they had been before the appointment, conversation on the way home was forced. None of us was able to speak about the real issue, so we talked about safe topics like the weather and what we were having for dinner. By the time we reached home Alex was buoyant. She ran off to her room while we took a walk and vented our feelings. We were exhausted, relieved—and mad as hell. If Alex thought that now that she was on the pill she could do anything she wanted, she had another think coming. We'd show *her*.

That evening we had several errands to run. Alex requested that we drop her off at the Boyfriend's house to watch TV, something she had done on several previous evenings.

But that was then and this was now. Before we were reasonable, flexible parents. Now we were:

THE SEX POLICE!!

Without verbalizing it, we both understood that our job was to make certain she and the Boyfriend had no opportunity for sex. So we began to question. What are your plans? Will his mother be home? Yes, our daughter said, clearly irritated by our inquisition.

But when we dropped her off, we learned the mother was *not* home. Put on the spot, exasperated and irritated, we bit the bullet and let her stay. Then we rushed through our errands at record speed and hurried back to the Boyfriend's house, our moods becoming blacker by the minute.

He walked her to the car, a smirk on his face. Seeing our dour expressions, he asked why we were so glum and told us to cheer up. Everything about him was so offensive to us at that moment that we could barely be civil. When we got home, the two of us conferred briefly and then told Alex we didn't want her bringing the Boyfriend to our home for a while. She responded with angry tears and slamming doors.

In the ensuing weeks the tension in our household hit record highs. It could be cut with a knife. The issue of sex hung in the air, creating stress, snappy tempers, an air of divisiveness.

The two of us knew we had to stand together or the whole household would fall apart, but finding the necessary compromise created constant conflict between us. As we struggled to find a mutual voice, we became strict with Alex, letting her know every way we could that we strongly disapproved of what she was doing and that we weren't going to change our minds about it.

Being the Sex Police was exhausting, but we stayed on her. When she went out, we asked, Where are you going? Who with? Will adults be there? We scrutinized. You have too much black eye makeup on. Where is the dance being held? Who are the chaperones? Where before there had been a reprimand, we now took away privileges for a variety of offenses: problems at school, talking back, not doing assigned chores.

We argued with her. "How can you say you have self-respect and self-control when you sleep with your boyfriend?"

"If I didn't have self-respect and self-control, I'd do it with the whole football team," she replied angrily.

Thinking she didn't get the message, we laid it on the line. "You're flouting our values. We do *not* believe in sex at sixteen!"

Seemingly without embarrassment she shot back at us, "I *like* sex. It's my body and I'm old enough to do what I want. Even if I break up with my boyfriend, I'll have sex with my next one, so you might as well get used to it!"

Fortunately, our other daughter continued on a steady course, busy with friends and school. While we had some problems with Marissa, she didn't seem to have the need to try all the things her sister was doing. Instead, she would observe what was going on, occasionally challenging us or demanding to know what was happening. We made sure she knew how much we disapproved of her sister's activities.

Even the night of the prom we would not relent and have the Boyfriend at the house. We never had the chance to see the two of them dressed up. She went to his house for photos and the send-off. She had talked us into a late curfew, and we tried not to think about all the stories we had heard of high school students checking into area motels after the dance.

Not long afterward we learned that the Boyfriend had visited our daughter in our own house in the middle of the night while we were sleeping soundly.

Furious, we grounded her and took away privileges yet again. More stress, more harsh words, more restless nights. Our nerves were frayed. We all had colds and the flu and tension headaches. Alex looked pale and had circles under her eyes. Marissa started dropping hints that she would like to move out, that our family wasn't any fun anymore.

It wasn't. We felt that we were losing control. We couldn't seem to reach Alex. She had no remorse, no guilt. We hated being the Sex Police. We weren't preventing her and the Boyfriend from having sex—we were merely forcing them to be more resourceful. We had approached his single-parent mother to see how she felt about it, but all she said was that she was aware that they were sleeping together and didn't think it was any big deal.

We were beginning to wonder if we were the only ones who thought it was. Were we completely out of touch with reality? We didn't think so. We'd both been around the block a few times, but casual sex was not something teenagers in our day thought they had a right to, and we didn't think they did today. What about the issues of right and wrong? Why had our daughter gone against the values she had been raised with? Why was she so blatant about her "right" to do this?

Her health was becoming more of a problem. Even though she was very slim, the Boyfriend told her she was too fat for his tastes. She began to starve herself in spite of anything we could say to her. She developed a stubborn upper respiratory infection and couldn't shake it. We attributed it to her smoking, poor eating and sleeping habits, and stress—some of which was due to his threats to break up with her because of our strict rules and some because of her constant conflicts with us.

Still trying to be reasonable about everything, we relented and allowed the Boyfriend to come over, first sitting down with him and telling him our objections to him and to our daughter's behavior since she had begun to date him. Alex was thrilled to have him back in the house, but whenever he was there or went on family outings with us, we were all tense.

We confided to a friend with an eighteen-year-old daughter about how upset we were. She listened sympathetically, then congratulated us that we'd gotten Alex to age sixteen before sex became an issue.

"I had to put my daughter on the pill at age thirteen," she revealed to our considerable amazement. "For a long time I felt like a failure as a parent. But I've finally accepted that it's just the way things are today. There's nothing you can do about it except what you've done, which is to help her protect herself. And you have to do that because few teenagers are capable of safely managing their sex lives. The other thing is to do whatever is necessary to be at peace with this issue. Because you're going to have to learn to live with it."

We tried to process her message. Was this how today's parents were handling the issue of teenage sex? *By learning to live with it?*

If that was, finally, what we had to do, at least we had to understand why it had happened. Could we have prevented it? What had we done wrong? If we had done nothing wrong, what forces had proved more powerful than our family value structure? We felt we had to know.

School was about to end for the summer. We knew that for our own sanity we needed some distance from Alex. We also reasoned that if she had some time away from the Boyfriend she might see him for what he was and lose interest in him. Above all, we wanted her to regain her self-esteem and her direction in life.

She wanted to visit family in New York, so we arranged for her to leave as soon as school was out. When we said we were unsure of a return date, she began to catch on and protested long and vehemently. She told us we were ruining her life and promised to be good if we would reconsider. We were adamant: We needed a break. She then began making plans for the Boyfriend to visit her. We chose not to respond to this and just hoped it wouldn't work out. We knew we couldn't stop it.

She wanted him to come to the airport with us. We told her we needed time for a private good-bye. They had a tearful parting, vowing to write and call every day and declaring that they would miss each other every minute.

Then we whisked her off to the airport, gave her a big hug, said we loved her—and watched to make sure she got on the plane before we turned to leave.

CHAPTER 2

HOW TEENS FEEL ABOUT LIFE AND LIBIDO

Even as Alex's plane was lifting into the air, we noticed how much better we could breathe. The body under stress doesn't breathe well.

The next thing we noticed was how nice it was to have some quality time with Marissa. Then she, too, left to visit relatives, and we settled into a few peaceful childless weeks in which to sort out what had happened to us and try to figure out what we were going to do about it.

When we were together, we were talking about it. How could parents and teenagers work through all the other issues that come up if they disagree on the very important topic of sexual activity? Were Alex's attitudes typical? Why had she so easily bypassed what we had taught her? We knew the statistics that over 50 percent of high school students are sexually active—70 percent of high school seniors. Were these other sexually active teenagers able to converse easily with their parents about this? Were they protecting themselves? Did they understand the dangers?

We happened to be visiting with Steve Walker, a county health department consultant who often works with students in the public schools. When we mentioned our concern and confusion to him, he suggested we find out for ourselves.

"I'm running some classes for teens this summer. Why don't you come talk to a group of students?" he suggested. "They're pretty open and will probably tell you anything you want to know. I think they'll talk to you about sex."

Intrigued, we took him up on his offer, and one bright summer morning we walked into a room full of high school students, ages fifteen and sixteen.

"We'd like to talk to you about sex," we told them. They'd been warned that we were coming, so none of them seemed too startled. "We're trying to find out how teenagers regard sex and sexuality and how you and your parents communicate about sex."

At first their answers were guarded and indirect. After all, we looked like their parents. Gradually, they warmed to the topic and began to open up. For two hours we mostly listened to these young people express their feelings and concerns.

"Today, with AIDS and all those diseases around, we have to be talking to our parents," a girl volunteered. "I think in my mom's day, anything about sex was kept real quiet. She's always saying, 'Don't you dare tell that to your grandmother.' But now people have to talk. It's embarrassing, but you have to do it."

"When Magic Johnson was on TV talking about AIDS, my mom sat down with me and my fourteen-year-old brother and watched it," another girl said. "That was the first time she ever mentioned sex to either one of us. She warned us that it's *trouble*. We knew she meant for us not to have sex, but both of us do. We wouldn't do it with anybody who's got AIDS, though."

"My mom has talked to me about the physical dangers and the emotional dangers of sex, but she said it was nice too," a third girl volunteered. "She got pregnant on her sixteenth birthday when she did it for the very first time. She had to get an abortion and she didn't know if she'd ever be able to have kids after that. It's real emotional for her. She tries to teach me that sex is not something you play around with, because she doesn't want me to have to go through that. She doesn't say she knows I have sex, but she probably does. She just says use a condom."

"I think the message in the movies is that it's okay to do it," a boy said. "We don't have to listen to parents. We know the problems, and we use protection."

"Then how come we all know at least one girl who's pregnant?" challenged a girl. "You guys don't use condoms and you know it. Probably most of us know someone with a sex disease, and before too long we'll know someone with AIDS."

"I have a close friend who's pregnant," another girl said. "I wanted to yell at her, 'Why didn't you use a condom?' But I didn't go off on her because it was over and done with. Besides, she's real happy about it."

"She didn't have to get pregnant," a boy said. "Girls should know how to protect themselves. The part about condoms is true, so it's up to the girls. They should be on the pill."

"Well, maybe not all girls can get them," a girl responded to him. "When you're going out with someone, you do what you want. If you're going to have sex, safe or unsafe, you just do it. You don't think about protection because you think, 'It's not going to happen to me.'"

"That's how my friends are," another boy replied. "You figure it won't happen the first time, or you'll pull out or something. You play Russian roulette. You only live once, so go ahead and do what you want. Don't give us rules."

"Parents are always giving out rules, but they're embarrassed to talk about sex. They won't answer your questions," another boy said. "They avoid it even if you try."

"There's no way I could talk to my parents about whether it's okay for me to do it with someone I really love. I already know what they'd say," replied a girl. "They'd say, 'At your age you can't really be in love with somebody and you shouldn't have sex.' "

"You can't trust your parents anyway," said a girl, her voice laced with animosity. "I was with my four-year-old niece and she asked her mom what a virgin was because she heard the word on television, and my aunt said something like 'It's a burp.' I would have told her the truth. Parents should tell the truth."

"Starting when?" someone asked.

"Real early," she replied. "Whenever they start asking questions about sex. You should tell them. Information should come from the parents instead of somebody else who might say something that isn't true and mess with the person emotionally. If your parents lie to you, then who can you trust?"

"Parents should get it set up so if the kid has a question, he can ask it and get a straight answer," agreed a boy. "You're supposed to answer. Parents shouldn't say, 'You don't need to know that till you're older.' I can understand if it's a four-year-old asking something bad, but teenagers should get honest answers."

"I disagree about giving information to little kids," a girl said. "I babysit a five-year-old who's such a little pervert. He knows the facts and he's nasty about it. He plays with the little girls in the neighborhood you know what I mean? His parents should tell him, 'That's not right. You have to wait.' He already knows too much for his own good. He's going to be a real jerk in a few years 'cause he already thinks he can have what he wants."

"A lot of my friends have never talked to their parents about sex," added a boy. "Everything else, but not that. But kids don't want to talk to them anyway. It's a drag. It's too embarrassing."

"Something has to happen before most parents get involved. They have to find a condom or something," a girl said. "It depends on the parents. Mine don't talk, but I have a girlfriend whose parents do talk. They seem comfortable about it. My friend tells them everything."

"Would she tell them she's having sex?" someone asked.

"Are you kidding?" The girl laughed. "She doesn't tell them about *that*. Would *you*? Parents can't handle that kind of stuff. What I meant was, they talk about sex, but just sort of in general. They don't know she does it."

"If you tell your parents, it causes big trouble," a boy said. "That happened to a friend of mine. After that they wouldn't even let her go out with friends. I think most parents are stupid about things like that. They give off that attitude that they don't think we have sex. That's fine with us. We just all play a big game. We all have sex, but they think we don't."

"So everyone keeps secrets from each other," someone stated.

"Yeah. Parents think we're too young for sex. Everybody else says it's okay, but you know how parents are. They all say, 'Wait till you get married.' "

"Some parents know kids don't wait," interjected a girl, "but they say, 'If you get pregnant or your girlfriend gets pregnant, don't come home.' Then what?"

"They say, 'If you do it, I'm going to be disappointed in you,' " another girl responded. "And if they won't let you come home, then where do you go? It's not like you can say, 'Mom and Dad, I'm going to start having sex and I want to know, if I get pregnant, will you be there for me?' You'd get locked up!"

"But they let us date, and everybody is doing it and you want to try it. Kissing and other stuff gets old, and besides, it's natural to do it," a boy said. "You can't stop. Things get pretty intense and the girl doesn't make you stop and then you just do it."

"I know I sometimes take chances. I wish I knew what my parents' attitude would be if I got pregnant," a girl said wistfully. "Would they be there for me? I wish I could ask them."

"You can't talk to parents about stuff like that," a girl said. "Most relationships break apart if they find out you're having sex. Parents need to deal with this. It isn't going to go away and they shouldn't just push it away. But we shouldn't push our parents away when they get in our face, because they're going to be there forever."

"I fought with my mom all the time about my boyfriend," another girl said. "Finally we sat down to talk about me having sex with my boyfriend because it was breaking both of us apart and putting us on edge. Sex was this really big issue between us. I told her, 'You and I are going to be around a lot longer than this guy is, so we have to talk about this.' "

"I'll bet she told you that you were too young," someone said.

"No. She just didn't want me to get hurt," the girl replied.

"Did she trust you?" someone else asked.

"She trusted me, but not the guy," the girl said, causing several students around her to laugh knowingly.

"My mom's a single parent and I'm close to her. I tell her everything," a girl volunteered. "I told her the first time I had sex. She asked if it was forced on me. She asked if I had questions and then she put me on the pill. So it just depends on the parent and the kid. My mom hasn't always liked guys I've done it with, but the thing is, she's usually right about them. She doesn't come right out and say it, though. I dated a real jerk last year. Mom never really said he was, but she asked me questions like, 'Do you like the way he treats you? Where do you think your relationship is going?' I found out she was a good judge of character."

"It's always moms. Dads can't talk about this stuff at all," a student observed. "They just make it clear you'd better not do it or else. Moms at least try to talk."

"My dad wants me to be his little angel," a girl said. "He calls me his baby. He cried when he saw the movie *Father of the Bride* and said how bad he was going to feel when my sister and I left him. He talked about us getting married and how he was our first love. It made me uncomfortable."

"I'm not even sure what a father's role is supposed to be," another girl responded. "I have a stepfather who's never home. I guess I have a television image about fathers, but real fathers aren't like that. Real fathers don't sit down and talk to you about things like sex." She turned to the boy seated next to her. "If you were a father, would you talk to your kids about sex?"

He looked momentarily startled, but then said, "If it was a girl, I'd have my wife talk to her. I'd listen to her, though. I don't want to be like my dad. My mom does all the emotional stuff. I just joke with my dad. We talk about cars. Anything else is real awkward, and if I ask him anything else, he just stands there and looks at me."

"What about you?" one of the students asked a teacher who was in the room. He responded immediately, "I tried to talk to my four-teen-year-old son about sex and he was out of the room in a flash. It's easier for me with my daughter, who's twelve, because she's more receptive. I think it's real important that you start whenever they ask questions so it becomes natural. I didn't do a good job of that with my son. But if you think this generation of males has problems, the last generation was a lot worse. So we're getting better. We fathers have to deal with our sons. We need to teach them they can't impose their sexual wishes on girls. Boys need to understand the boundary between consensual sex and date rape. Fathers have to get involved. Moms can't explain that stuff to guys."

"But it still drives me nuts that most of the time parents don't think we're old enough or smart enough to think for ourselves," a boy said. "They say, 'You're not old enough to know what you're getting into,' 'You're not old enough to see that you shouldn't do this,' or 'You're not old enough to make this kind of decision.' "

"Maybe we make mistakes, but they have to let us learn from that," another boy said. "After all, they did. They've been through it. They can give options, but then they've got to let us learn on our own. Or else when they aren't there anymore, we won't be able to do it on our own. This is a problem for everyone I know. If parents do talk to you, they usually wait until it's too late. And by then you don't feel you can talk to them, because they're going to get mad if they find out what you're doing."

"My dad treats my sister different than me," the boy sitting next to him said. "He keeps an eye on her. Guys can have sex with several girls, but girls can't do that or they're sluts. Parents give guys more freedom and put more pressure on girls. It's wrong. Guys can talk to their moms, but girls can't talk to their dads. They don't want their dads to know they're interested in sex. If my father thought I was having sex, he'd probably just try to give me some advice. But if he thought my sister was doing it, he'd lock her up."

"Get real. Boys don't get pregnant," a girl responded.

"But they still might have to support a baby, and they might catch something. Most of us just hear 'Don't get caught.' I think we need more information than that," he replied.

"I think most parents are hypocrites," another girl added. "Mine are. They say, 'Don't do it,' but they don't tell you when you can do it and they won't help, so there's no communication."

"If I ask my parents a question, they right off think I'm doing it," a boy said. "I go to my older brother or a friend instead. Parents love you and should be honest with you, but they send out these waves that say, 'Don't come near me with this question.' Friends try to give good advice but they may not know the right answers."

"I'm going to be different when I'm a parent," a girl said. "Sex is part of being human, yet everyone clams up. AIDS makes it important. I'm going to talk openly about it. Don't judge. Tell them the truth."

"Parents try to make you think they were perfect and made no mistakes. They just don't want us to know what they did as teenagers because they think it'll be giving us permission to do the same thing."

"I wish I could know what my folks were really like as teenagers," a girl said reflectively. "I've asked them but they make it sound like they were real good all the time and I don't know if they're telling the truth or not. I don't think they can remember anymore. If they could remember, maybe they'd be more sympathetic to what I go through."

"I think it's the opposite," another girl said. "They're strict *because* they remember what they did as teenagers. They don't think we have the right to make our own mistakes. They had good times and now they won't let us have good times."

"And they want us to have their values, but I want my own values. They can't think for me," the first replied.

If you could give parents of teenagers some realistic advice, what would it be? we asked.

"Give us real information," one girl said immediately. "Help us get good information about birth control, because otherwise there may be pregnancy or disease. Be straightforward."

"Parents need to be reminded that they're different from their kids," said another girl, "and we're different from one another. They should talk to other parents instead of just making up their minds by themselves."

"But don't worry about other parents," a boy interjected. "And be open with your kids. Give them more facts. Let your kids talk to you if they need to talk."

"Parents should also keep their eyes open, because some parents act like nothing can happen to their kids," said a girl. "They don't do *anything* for their kids. They just don't care."

"Don't try to avoid my questions. If I say I really like this guy, is there a way for me to have safe sex with him? Tell me," another girl said. "Don't just tell me I shouldn't have sex, because I'm going to anyway."

"Don't make a difference between sons and daughters," replied the boy who had brought up this issue. "The double standard isn't fair."

"Understand what it's like to be a teenager. Too many parents have forgotten," said a girl. "Take time out to talk to your kids about their worries. Realize that they *have* worries."

We looked at a boy in the back row who had been quiet throughout the discussion and asked him if he'd like to give a message to his parents. "Yes," he said softly. "While I'm going through all this, let me know you care. Be my friend. You think I don't want that because I don't act like I do, but you know what? That's what I need most from you. Just be my friend."

Our heads were full of these young people when we left. We went out for coffee to talk about them and found ourselves comparing what they'd said about their parents with what we had done with Alex and Marissa.

One of their key messages was that teenagers are going to have sex whether or not it's okay with their parents—and yet they want to communicate about sex with their parents. They want help. They want honest information. They *don't* want to be judged or controlled or discounted.

But parents can't do that, we argued. Parents must not lose control. Kids need structure and supervision. Parents can't let their children know how fallible they are and how many mistakes they've made themselves. Parents are *supposed* to be models of correct behavior.

The issue of control is a major one. Parents don't want to give it up until they're sure their teen can handle it, and teenagers are going to do everything they can to get it. They *have* to in order to become individuals. We could feel these teens' desire for closeness to their parents, and at the same time we understood their need to break free of their parents and make their own decisions. Not a single one of them had suggested that there might be something wrong with teenagers' having sex. They weren't asking their parents' permission for something they felt they had a right to do, but they also didn't want to disappoint their parents. They didn't want to make dangerous mistakes, and they needed their parents to help them.

It's never been easy being a teenager—we could remember plenty of conflicts from our own teen years—but it seems harder today, and not just because of sex.

We began to talk about the kind of world we are giving over to these young people. Our heritage had been Vietnam, Watergate, a decayed urban infrastructure, and nuclear warheads. We are passing along a depleted ozone layer, out-of-control national debt, overcrowded prisons, AIDS, and the fractured American family.

Yes, women are making progress in the war for equality, and yes, there are exciting advances happening in medical research, and yes, we're learning much about our universe from space exploration. But we knew from our own kids and from reading articles about today's teen that they don't have the optimism and the belief in America and its future that we had when John F. Kennedy told us to ask not what our country could do for us, but what we could do for our country.

Teenagers today are more cynical, more jaded, less hopeful about a future in which overpopulation and pollution are compromising the quality of life all over the globe.

In spite of this, if you ask teenagers what they want, they won't sound a whole lot different from how we did in the sixties. In response to the question "What do you want most in life?," six girls in the ninth grade said:

"To get along with my parents."

"For life to be safe in the future."

"For my boyfriend and me to last forever."

"Money, looks, and a car."

"Trust from everybody."

"Great legs."

If you ask them what they worry most about, the list generally looks like this:

1. parent dying
2. nuclear war
3. poor grades
4. their own death
5. illness, disability, or accident
6. not finding a satisfying job
7. world hunger
8. being a victim of a violent crime
9. nuclear-power-plant accident
10. getting cancer

What do teenagers want? Security, love, trust, money, great legs. What do teenagers worry about? Death, hunger, crime, illness. They worry about not having control, about not having choices, about being victims. Just as adults do. Life is complex for teenagers. Many of us adults view them as enjoying a hedonistic lifestyle with no worry about taxes, about keeping a job in spite of the recession, or about making ends meet on a limited budget. They have great bodies, they have fun—in short, they're carefree.

But few teens feel carefree. Already, at ages fifteen, sixteen, and seventeen, they feel old. They look back at their childhoods with a mixture of longing ("Life was so much more simple then"), regret ("I wish I'd been nicer to that shy kid who sat by himself at lunch"), and nostalgia ("Remember how much fun we had at recess?").

They feel insecure and inadequate. They worry that they might be gay because they have a crush on a same-sex teacher. They can't forget the trauma of falling up the steps in front of everybody on their way to American History, or of how they wanted to fade into the woodwork when a huge pimple popped out on their nose, and they're still recovering from the heartbreak they suffered when the boy or girl they liked from afar went with someone else to the ninth-grade dance.

Most of us suffered from some or all of those same anxieties. As wonderful as first-time love can be, and as special as memories of fun with friends can be, few of us, if actually given the opportunity, would choose to be sixteen again. The teenage years are just too hard. Too unsure, too traumatic, and for many teens, too hopeless.

Crusty old philosophers tell us that youth is wasted on the young, and crusty old songwriters tell us that love is wasted on the young. We wish we could be as healthy, strong, and slim as we were when we were eighteen, we wish we could stay up half the night partying with friends and still feel good the next day, we wish our skin could be as smooth and our eyes as bright and clear as they were those many years ago. But don't forget the pressure you felt to make good grades, to coexist in a family, to look just right and act just right, to be in the right clique, to attract the attention of that boy or girl you liked, to make decisions about your future, to deal with your powerlessness, to make the team, to take all those college entrance exams, to get into the college of your choice, to qualify for a scholarship. By contrast, holding a job and paying your taxes may sound easier.

Just dealing with your day-to-day emotional swings could be exhausting. Up one day, down the next. Feelings could even change from hour to hour.

A close friend of ours had reminded us of this in writing of her own teenhood in the late 1960s and early 1970s:

Back then we all thought that all the great ideas had been discovered by our generation and that previous generations were idiots. No one had ever experienced love like we were experiencing it. No one understood sorrow like we did.

I would lay on the couch crying because the world was so-o-o-o sad. I had two volumes—regular and my full-blown you-don't-understand-me scream. If Mom asked me how the party was, I would respond, "Why? Do you think we were doing something wrong?" If she wanted to know what I did in school, I felt she was prying. I wasn't always like that—a lot of [the] time I was giggly and goofy—but there was always an underlying feeling that my parents didn't trust me. And as I pushed the limits of sexual experience, my guilt and fear of getting caught also fueled my hostility toward them. My parents didn't know my boyfriend and I were having sex. Had they found out and forbidden me to see him, I would have done everything in my power to see him anyway. I remember thinking that I was an adult trapped in a world full of rules for children.

I wish so much importance wasn't put on sex. It starts out as a terrible dark secret loaded down with guilt and taboos and branded with a neon sign that flashes EVIL.

Then we get married and suddenly sex, which we've been thinking all this time is rotten and evil, is supposed to be this terrific thing we do all the time. I know I would be a lot less inhibited if sex had been treated casually as a part of life.

But when our friend slept with her boyfriend, she *knew* she was doing something she shouldn't. The point of crossover from good to bad was absolutely clear. Teenagers today have a different kind of problem: Society expects them to have sex. They may know for a fact that their parents would disapprove of their having sex, but as part of their attempt to break away from their parents' control, they may discount this. The message from their churches may be to wait, but too often the stronger message from friends and the culture around them is "Do it!" Given how much emphasis our culture puts on sex, it's amazing there are any teenage virgins left in this country.

That aspect of being a teenager is different from what it was for us. Other things are the same. Teenagers still spend their money on themselves, typically on food, transportation, entertainment, clothes, and items such as watches and cameras. Only one in four saves for college or other long-term objectives. Just as we did, they have their own fashions. Just as we did, they decorate their rooms with posters of rock stars, invest in cassette tapes or CDs, watch sitcoms on TV, torment younger siblings, resist doing assigned chores, listen to loud music while they study, and talk as long on the phone as parents will allow.

In addition to their often faulty thinking, their bodies are awkward, their appetites bottomless, their voices unreliable, their moods changeable. They can be alternately mouthy and shy, sweet and rude, mature and immature, idealistic and pessimistic, reliable and unreliable—all within the course of an hour or two!

Various studies and polls tell us that:

▶ Of 500 thirteen- to seventeen-year-olds who participated in a nationwide survey in 1991, 75 percent said that they thought religion was important and that they try to follow religious teachings.[1]

▶ Of 1,200 members polled by the National Association of Student Councils, 46 percent said alcohol is their school's most serious problem, followed by apathetic students; 51 percent of them drink liquor, 18 percent use marijuana, 8 percent have used cocaine or crack, and 67 percent have had sex. Of those who know their teachers' salaries, 78 percent said they were too low. Of those polled, 37 percent said a successful marriage will be most important to them as adults; 26 percent said career success, 20 percent said acquiring knowledge, and 11 percent said making money. Finally, 48 percent of them said they're most influenced by parents' opinions, while 34 percent were most influenced by classmates and 5 percent by teachers.[2]

▶ Teens spend an average of 25.6 percent of their time alone, according to a University of Chicago study. Overall, 41 percent of their lives is spent at home, 32 percent at school, and 27 percent in "public" places, such as in cars, in parks, or on the streets with their friends. They spend one-third of their day talking, and 13 percent of that time they are on the phone. Altogether, they spend 42 hours a week on leisure activities, which include socializing, 16 percent; watching television, 7.2 percent; nonschool reading, 3.5 percent; sports and games, 3.4 percent; and listening to music, 1.4 percent.[3]

So some things have changed—cocaine use, percentage who have had sex—and other things, like leisure-time activities, haven't.

Adults still have fits about their teenagers' decision-making abilities, just as our parents did. We have occasionally wondered if our daughters alighted on Planet Earth from some distant star. "What was she *thinking?*" we asked each other when one daughter emptied her savings account to buy an expensive Christmas present for a boyfriend she broke up with a month later. "Where was her *brain?*" we questioned when the other daughter smuggled a bottle of beer into a church youth group get-together—and promptly got caught and ejected from the party.

Maybe the word *teenager* should be changed to *betweenager* to describe these young people we love so much but often don't understand as they tumble headlong through the difficult transition between childhood and adulthood.

And now, where were we? Talking to other teenagers was reassuring. We liked them a lot and we appreciated their struggles, even if we didn't agree with their attitudes about sex.

But even if we now realized that all teens were struggling for autonomy, we were hardly ready to step aside and let Alex take control of her life. As much as we understood her need to separate from us, we also knew that as her parents, we had to make sure it happened in a safe, orderly fashion. Her choice of the Boyfriend certainly didn't indicate that she was ready to take on adult life without some guidance from us.

As to how to resolve our conflicts with her, we still needed guidance ourselves.

CHAPTER 3

PARENTS GET
THEIR TURN

Even if Alex's interest in sex and her decision to become
sexually active weren't crazy, we felt our reaction to her behavior
wasn't either.

But we were getting confused. From the beginning we had wondered if any other parents felt the same way we did. How were other
parents managing to tread these dangerous waters? Were we all struggling this hard with our teens over the issue of sex?

Since talking to teenagers had been so revealing, we reasoned that
we might find similar insight in talking with other parents of teenagers.

We drove to nearby Lawrence, Kansas, where we had formerly
lived. It's one of those wonderful Midwestern university communities
distinguished by liberal thinkers, ex-hippies, and interesting people.
At our request, a friend who is a massage therapist at a health collective
and who is the mother of teenagers called some other parents together—some we knew and some we didn't—and one sunny Sunday
afternoon we all made ourselves comfortable on futons and rocking
chairs in the collective's meeting room to share herbal tea and
conversation.

We hadn't known what to expect. What we found was that both mothers and fathers were willing—even eager—to talk, and that sex and teenagers is a powder-keg topic for parents.

"Recently the motel owners here got together and said they wouldn't rent rooms to teenagers anymore after events like the prom, because there had been so much destruction," one parent began. "What surprised me wasn't the destruction, but that teenagers had even been allowed to get rooms. Wow! I ran with a pretty wild crowd when I was a teenager, but *none* of us ever rented a motel room. No wonder these kids are having sex!"

"I always think I'm liberal, but I can't believe how much times have changed," the woman sitting next to her said. "I have a friend with four teenage sons who jokes that if she put a condom machine in the boys' bathroom she would make enough money to pay for their school lunches. She's *glad* they use condoms, but she's not at all happy about their level of sexual activity. Her youngest boy is only fourteen."

"When our son was a fourth-grader," a father said, "he told us that a sixth-grade girl had called him and offered in very graphic terms to have sex with him. We had thought we had lots of time before we started to deal with issues involving sex, but we started at that moment. Like you said, times have changed."

"Intellectually my husband and I made a choice to begin talking to our daughter about sex when she was very young," a mother said slowly. "We always tried to be open with her. The three of us even went through a parent-child sex-education course together. But she became sexually active at fifteen and it devastated us. We worried that we had taught her too much. We felt she wasn't mature enough to make what we considered to be one of the most important decisions of her life. The irony is that we've always been very careful to see that she got all the proper immunizations and the best of medical care. And then she went to one of those clinics by herself and they put her on the pill. She had only been menstruating a year and we worry about the long-term effects it might have on her body."

"I think your daughter did the right thing," a mother said to her. "I'm impressed that when she decided she was ready for sex she was responsible enough to go to a clinic and get protection. I would rather a girl did that than get pregnant."

"You sound like you're speaking from experience," someone commented.

"I am. My daughter got pregnant when she was sixteen. I had no idea she was having sex. I didn't give her a chance to even think about what to do after she told me. She had an abortion the next day. Looking back, I don't know if that was the right choice for the long run because she's had a lot of guilt about it, but it was for the short run. I think this issue of sex is so tough for families because we don't have community and media support of our values."

"The media stabs you in the back," another mother agreed. "To try to get my thirteen-year-old to read more, I told him I'd buy him a magazine subscription. He chose *Sports Illustrated*. My husband warned me about the swimsuit issue, but I didn't think it was any big deal. When that issue arrived, I didn't know how to deal with it. It was soft porn. This is a magazine that rarely shows women, and when it does, they've got their butts up in the air. I was very upset with what I saw as the exploitation of women in a men's magazine. My son loved the issue and thought I overreacted. I considered tearing out the offending pages, but my son told me he saw far worse things all the time, and I know he does."

"Have you listened to the lyrics of their music?" another parent asked. "It's violent and sexist and graphic. I hate my kids' music, but I let them play it as long as they keep it low enough that I can't hear it. I know that otherwise they'll just buy the tapes and hide them from me."

"I agree it's horrible," a father responded. "My son says, 'Listening to this doesn't make me a bad person. I listen, but I know better.' I wish I believed that."

"Kids have to rebel somehow," a parent reminded him, "especially the ones who come from real stable homes. They feel stifled and have to break away from parental control. It's part of being a teenager."

"Their rebellion can be tough on everyone," a mother said. "One of my daughters was sexually active quite young and sometimes the guys were real creeps. But that paled next to her running away for periods of time when she was fourteen and fifteen. It was awful not knowing where she was or if she was okay. We were on an emotional roller coaster with the schools all the time. The police were indifferent. She always had places to stay—you'd be amazed at how many parents let runaways stay at their homes. I would have traded all of that in an instant to have had her home and sexually active with a boyfriend I couldn't stand."

"I agree they're going to rebel—we did against our parents, too— but trying to give them necessary information so they don't get seriously hurt can be a real problem," a mother sighed. "My husband tried to talk to our son about sex and birth control and didn't feel he got anywhere. No matter what my husband said, our son would respond, 'Oh, I know that.' Kids today go for the spontaneity of experiences. Yet they don't know what they're doing and they think they're invincible. You can't convince them that smoking is a delayed time bomb or that if they don't practice safe sex they could get AIDS. They don't think they have to say no to anything."

"We thought casual teaching was going to be the best approach with our kids, conveying our values along with the hard information they need," a father said. "It hasn't worked well. We can't do it at the dinner table because there's a twelve-year-old difference in ages from our oldest to youngest and all levels of development and experience in between. Since my wife is home more, she's likely to react to something they see on television and use that as an opportunity for discussion, but those opportunities don't come up too often."

"Difficult issues are easier to deal with if you're not married," a mother said. "I'm single now. It's much simpler to handle the kids on my own and not worry about what my husband will think and how problems with the kids will affect our relationship."

"Married or not, I think support from other parents is the key," another mother commented. "You can't count on the schools or the community. You're lucky if you have relatives in town who will help. If you don't, let your kids know you talk to other parents. I do this regularly with other mothers. My daughter calls it 'the Mommy Connection.' She understands its power. She knows I know more than what she tells me because the mothers pool information and give each other support. You need that if you're having problems with your kid."

"Sometimes you just have to be reminded that what these kids are doing is normal and that they're good kids," added another parent. "Twenty years from now they'll probably be sitting here trying to figure out *their* kids. But all of this would be easier if both parents and teenagers weren't so embarrassed talking about sex."

"Actually, I'm not sure anything embarrasses them," a mother said. "The other day one of my nineteen-year-old daughter's girlfriends was at our house talking to me about a sexual experience that was upsetting for her. She was very open about it all, very explicit. On the other hand, when I said, 'Can you go home and talk to your mom about this?' she said no. I guess she wanted to talk to someone of her mother's generation, but not to her mom."

"I'd be glad to talk to my sons' friends about sex," another mother said wistfully. "One of my sons spent several hours talking to a friend's mother the other day. It hurts me that he didn't come to me, but I know that unless it's a real drastic situation he probably isn't going to. When you try to talk to your own children, judgments get in the way and you shut down immediately."

"Discussing sexual experiences with your children almost goes against the incest taboo. It's real primal. No wonder we can't do it," another parent added.

"It's too highly charged an issue," a father said. "Parents are afraid that if they talk frankly about sex, their kids will do it. It also makes kids mad if we assume they are having sex when they aren't. I know one parent that backfired on. She gave her daughter a box of condoms, which made the daughter angry. Her parents were entertaining company one evening and the daughter came in the room and asked her mother very loudly where the condoms were."

"But," a parent said slowly, "even if parents can't talk to their teenagers about sex, with all the information out there, surely kids know everything they need to know."

"They're knowledgeable by the book," a mother responded. "They know the plumbing. But when it comes to issues about being responsible and planning ahead, then they're not very knowledgeable at all."

"They have the information, they have the mechanics of it, and that's all," another added. "It takes time for the deeper knowledge to develop. They think such stupid things."

As the group began to break up, two parents continued this discussion.

"You can't trust the schools to get the information to them. Kids dismiss that. They talk to their friends, but their friends may not know the truth," one father said, with a shrug. "You know teenagers—the dumb things they do and believe are amazing."

The other father nodded in agreement. "They're like toddlers who know words but don't know what they mean," he said. "When it comes to sex, teenagers know the talk, they know the walk, but they don't know how to put the talk and the walk together. Somehow as their parents we're supposed to help them learn, when half the time we can't stand them and we can't stand the things they do. Now how do you reconcile all that—and still stay friends with your kid?"

We headed home, comforted to know that other parents were struggling too, but with little real information to help us with Alex. Maybe other parents couldn't help us. Or maybe the Lawrence group wasn't representative of all parents. Before drawing conclusions, we wanted to talk to more parents. We approached a suburban Kansas City parenting group with the same request: that we hear their concerns about teenagers and sex. The group leaders questioned us at length. Once they decided our motives were sincere, they agreed to visit with us.

The common denominator of the group, most of whom were mothers, was that each member had a child who would be a junior in the fall at the same high school. They met in one another's homes to discuss topics of mutual concern. Unlike our tie-dyed, Birkenstock-shod group in Lawrence, these were designer-label-sportswear folks. That aside, the issues were similar—though, not surprisingly, their reactions were more conservative.

"Kids today know everything about sex," began one mother. "When I was a teenager, I firmly believed that if I had sex I'd get pregnant and ruin my life. I don't think there are any mysteries left about sex for teenagers today like there were for us."

"I knew about sex but I also knew it wasn't for me," another mom responded. "Life seemed so innocent then. I remember when I was a college senior in 1968 and I filled out a questionnaire that asked whether I'd ever smoked pot. I didn't know *anybody* in college who smoked pot."

"For me, having a beer at a college party was a big deal,"confirmed another mother. "But some things weren't as good. We thought we had to be married by the time we got out of college. Today kids are putting off marriage. I think that's good. They'll make better choices."

"But we got married so young because that was the only legitimate way we could have sex. Today they don't have to wait," the woman sitting next to her responded. "In fact, they don't have to wait for *anything*. They don't *ever* have to marry. They can have sex, live together, have children together—things we absolutely couldn't do without marriage. Five girls at our middle school right now—this is confirmed—have sexually transmitted diseases. These are seventh-, eighth-, and ninth-graders!

"It's probably the first time they've encountered something that doesn't have an easy solution," she continued. "Kids are so used to quick fixes. You don't like the teacher, you switch classes. You smash your car, your folks get it fixed for you. You get pregnant, you get an abortion. The focus is the child. It's the child-centered family."

"It's hard work for parents to keep kids focused, and then it can backfire," reflected one mom. "My son has a friend who started soccer in second grade. He had his choice of five soccer scholarships to college and he turned them down because he was completely burned out on soccer. All these activities we get our kids into, and then we have to drive them everywhere because we live in the suburbs and they can't walk to anything. Family life has changed."

"Churches have changed, too," the lone father in the group said. "What's happened to the concept of sin? We grew up with this clear line between right and wrong. It doesn't exist anymore. We were sensitive about embarrassing our parents. Today, dads pay the parking tickets for kids and moms go yell at the school administrators when the kid gets in trouble. We were much more respectful of adults when I was young."

"My daughter told me of an incident where a freshman boy told the freshman basketball coach to 'shut up.' The coach kicked him off the team and the mom called the varsity coach and complained," related one mother. "The next day the boy was back on the team. What kind of message does that send kids?"

"They aren't just rude to adults," said another. "At the school talent show I couldn't believe how badly they acted toward the performers. They talked through the show and ridiculed the kids on stage, and at least half the student audience left before the show was over."

"But parents aren't any better," another mother added. "I questioned one mother about her decision to rent a hotel room for her daughter and her daughter's date on prom night. I was very nice about it. She told me to mind my own business. I'm tired of defending my values, yet I'm so unsure at what point I must compromise my values and cave in to the demands of society or whatever the social norm is today. How far can I give?"

"I don't get it. Are we trying to save our children from what we suffered?" questioned a parent. "Sometimes I ask myself why I cleaned up all that spilled milk for my kids. My son won't accept responsibility for his actions. My husband's never around, and I'm the only stabilizing force. I'm real frustrated. I don't know what's going to happen to this boy."

"Consequences were different for us," another mother said. "I'm bothered by this thing about teens checking into hotel rooms after the prom. I grew up in a little town and we were always told, *"Don't go to the river!"* One night a girlfriend and I were picked up by two older guys and of course that was where we went—and the next day the whole town knew about it. *Every*body knew. If my mother didn't know about something I was doing, one of my friends' mothers did and immediately told her. If I'd checked into a hotel with a guy, I would have had to leave town in disgrace."

The woman across from her brought up another point. "My daughter's shy and doesn't have a boyfriend. I think part of the reason, based on the few things she's said, is that she doesn't feel ready for sex, and if you date a boy more than a few times, sex is expected. Girls today can't date around. If you do, you have a bad reputation because the expectation is that you have sex with every boy you go out with."

Said another, "But so many girls don't say no. When we were teenagers, boys were expected to be aggressive and girls were expected to set the limits. We've all taught our daughters to be assertive, and today the girls are as aggressive as the boys when it comes to sex. My son who's in grade school gets suggestive calls from girls, for heaven's sake. What boy turns down a sure thing? Boys can feel real pressured to have sex. Girls will accuse them of being fags if they *won't* do it."

"But birth control wasn't available for us," someone added. "Guys couldn't even get condoms and the pill wasn't that available yet— and doctors weren't giving it to teens without parental consent anyway. Removing the fear of pregnancy has made a huge difference."

"Back in college," said another, "you were put on probation if you went to a guy's room. Today they have coed dorms and twenty-four-hour visitation in the rooms. Fraternities at the state university have out-of-town overnight parties. They all drive to St. Louis for the weekend. Happens all the time."

"That kind of behavior starts so early," another mother said, nodding in agreement. "We're hearing about eighth-grade parties where the parents permit smoking and drinking. Then there are the junior-high and senior-high coed slumber parties. Supposedly everybody's just friends, and nothing happens, but the last one I heard about, the parents told other parents they'd stay visible. Instead, once ten P.M. rolled around, the kids didn't see them again until breakfast."

"Alcohol is often a factor in indiscriminate sex," the father said. "It cloaks kids' judgment and they're not using birth control and then you have problems. Drugs contribute, too. We have a serious drug problem at our high school. The kids can get LSD for three dollars a hit, cocaine for five to ten dollars a gram. Angel dust is readily available. Easy alcohol, easy drugs, easy sex. They can have it all."

"The values are crazy," another chimed in. "They can skip school and the administration does nothing about it. They can abuse their teachers and nothing happens. Although they can't be given an aspirin at school or get their ears pierced without parental permission, they can get an abortion and the parents never know about it."

"As parents, part of our responsibility is to protect them," a mother said. "I'm going to confess that I put my daughter on the pill last year. I just didn't want anything to happen to her."

"You were smart," said another. "We have good friends whose son got a girl pregnant and he has to pay child support. They told us that if we thought there was even a glimmer of a chance that my daughter might have sex to put her on the pill—which I have. My daughter has a steady boyfriend and I talked to her about it, and we made the decision together to do that."

"You've given her permission to have sex. What's happened to telling kids to wait until they're in love?" someone questioned.

"But they *do* think they're in love," chimed in a stylishly dressed mother. "They think they're in love with each person they have sex with. Teenagers fall in love very easily. Especially the girls."

Another mother jumped in, "Where did society get so far off track? If you're going to have coed slumber parties in junior high and dates check into hotels after the prom and you have twenty-four-hour visitation in the dorms, you're going to have sex. Society is setting them up. We're setting them up. Our parents didn't allow those things. Maybe we should teach chastity as a choice. Teach values and choices, and this is one and it's okay. I tell my son this. The messages to have sex are everywhere. Kids are bombarded. But you say, 'Yes, that's all out there, but saying no can be a choice too. You'll be better off in many ways. There are moral issues, health issues, psychological issues. You want a sex relationship to be nurturing and lifelong. If you start real young and get rejected, you'll wonder what's wrong with you.' I think kids can understand that."

"I told my son to fall in love with his right hand," deadpanned another to general laughter among the group. "I'm serious. I told him if these sexual urges were really on his mind, to masturbate. That's what guys have always done, that's what they did in our day, and they all seem to be pretty functional today. I told him to wait and have sex in a loving relationship. I told him to save himself for that."

"But it can still be an issue," another responded. "I have a daughter in her mid-twenties who thinks she's in a loving relationship. I know that she and her boyfriend have sex and I'm not comfortable with it. I've let her know that. I guess that's all I can do."

"But can you blame her for sleeping with him?" a woman asked. "Today it's like it's considered a curse to be a virgin. Girls wonder what's wrong with them. Boys, too. It's the exact opposite of our day. Talking about love and whether a girl should sleep with her boyfriend is almost a luxury. Parents need to admit that their teenagers are probably going to be sexually active and they need to see that they have protection. Because AIDS is out there and teenagers are getting it more and more. There was a rumor going around that a girl who was a senior last year has AIDS and she gave health officials a list three pages long of all the guys she had slept with."

"All this sex," one mother fumed, "but they just do it to do it. They don't know what good sex is."

"Where do I sign up for a course in good sex?" a mother joked. "My husband and I need that."

"Why should we care if it's good for them? Let them fumble around like we did," one mother said, with a touch of bitterness in her voice. "If you start telling them that sex is wonderful and all that, then you're condoning it. I told my daughter that the physical side of sex may not be so good, but that sex can be a wonderful emotional experience—provided you're married. They have unreal expectations about it. So much of the sex in movies is violent or else the woman has earth-shaking orgasms."

"Most women fake orgasm," observed another mother. "What's important is that they see intimacy between their parents and learn from them that there's more to love than sex."

"But what's intimacy?" the woman sitting next to her asked. "Fathers spend minutes a day with their children. My husband and the kids barely know each other. The only kind of role model he is for them is work, work, work."

"Maybe that's the problem," someone observed. "There are no good parenting models anymore. The kids don't bond with their parents. Businesses give three to six weeks' maternity leave and that's it. Children grow up in day-care centers and as latchkey kids and so the girls have babies in order to have someone to love and to love them."

As the group began to break up, one mother approached us.

"I didn't want to say anything in front of the others because most of them know my daughter, but I wanted to tell you what's happened at our house," she said in a low voice. "My daughter Beth, who's now sixteen, had been dating her boyfriend almost a year and told me very bluntly that she felt ready to have sex. She was hoping I would put her on the pill but made it clear that she was going ahead whether I put her on the pill or not. I told her I felt she was too young and should wait, but she informed me that lots of her girlfriends were having sex and she's heard how wonderful it is.

"I tried to talk to my husband about it but he wouldn't even discuss it. Finally I took her to our doctor and she started the pill. My husband was very angry, and things just haven't been the same since. He says his heart breaks every time he looks at Beth, knowing what she's doing. He won't even speak to her boyfriend and leaves the room if the boy is at our house.

"I know Beth is a good girl, but it used to be that good girls didn't do this. I was a virgin until a month before my wedding. The only man I've ever had sex with is my husband. I'll admit that I was real close to doing it several times with boyfriends, but it was taboo and I didn't cross the line. Girls today think their mothers didn't have all those feelings. Of course we did! Nothing's changed—except that they do it and we didn't.

"My husband holds me responsible for all this. He wants Beth tested for AIDS. There's no reason because she and her boyfriend were each other's first. My husband tells me to 'watch those two like a hawk' when they're in the house together, but if I know they're having sex, isn't that hypocritical?

"The stress with my husband is getting more serious," she said sadly. "It's caused a real rift in what I thought was a very solid marriage, because it raises issues of trust and mistrust. I don't know what's going to happen to us."

Another mother walked with us to our car when we were leaving. "We're really messed up as a society," she said, shaking her head. "We've tried to give our children everything and now they expect it. They're ungrateful. They don't known the meaning of the word 'no.' Today you were talking to concerned parents who try hard and none of us knows what to do. Just think of all the kids floating around out there whose parents don't even care about them. I think the American family is doomed."

We weren't ready to go that far. Not doomed, we assured each other, just changing. Everything is changing in today's fast-paced world. While it may be happening a little too fast for our tastes, we certainly weren't ready to give up on the younger generation. We just wanted to understand it and help it.

We got together to share a glass of wine with Damon Montford, a family-practice physician and the single father of two daughters, one in her late teens and one in her early twenties. Like us, he'd had some parenting problems. Like us, he was trying to come to grips with sex and modern American society. As a physician, he often sees families wrestling with their adolescents and their desire to "grow up too quickly," as he put it.

"When drugs or sex becomes an issue, I've often seen all family communication break down," he said. "Parents fight with their kids about everything else, when one of these two things is really the issue. But parents may refuse to see it. Sometimes I have to be the one to tell them what's happening."

In order to get family members to talk to each other, he has sometimes recommended that they put the television sets away for a month and then return to him.

"If they'll do that, they'll start to talk again," he said. "Communication gets stronger. They'll gradually make breakthroughs. When they come back to me, often they've worked out their troubles. I think lack of communication is the biggest problem we have within the family structure."

On occasion he has had parents request that he talk to their teenagers about "the facts of life."

"But that's tough because the kids look at me and they see their fathers. They stare at the far wall and it's clear they aren't hearing me. I can't do parents' work for them."

Damon says frankly that few medical schools prepare physicians to handle these kinds of problems. Many don't even require that their graduates have exposure to psychiatry or the kinds of family therapy available to people with problems.

Like every physician, he's disturbed when he see young pregnant teenagers, which is happening more and more.

"I firmly believe that sex is the cement of any long-term relationship. I've taught my daughters that. When kids use it for sport or entertainment, that's not right. I'm not sure how we teach our young people that early sex is inappropriate."

In order to try to gain more insight into what parents could do, we decided to contact Dennis Dailey, a professor of social welfare at the University of Kansas who teaches a wildly popular course called Human Sexuality in Everyday Life. Since sex and culture is his area of expertise, maybe, we thought, he could enlighten us. It was worth a try.

We called for an appointment, and a few days later we went to see him.

CHAPTER 4

DENNIS DAILEY TOSSES US A HAND GRENADE

Dr. Dailey is a bearded, wiry Midwesterner, verbal, occasionally verbose, and equally able to inspire or outrage. He gets so excited to make his point that he frequently interrupts, peppering his speech with colorful language and hand gestures for emphasis. In another life he might have been a salty sea captain.

He and his wife are the parents of two twentysomething daughters, one married, one not. He is a professor in the School of Social Welfare at the University of Kansas and is a respected marriage and family therapist and sex educator who regularly publishes academic articles. He has been interviewed in the popular press and on television talk shows many times.

We knew he often worked with teenagers and had hosted a radio call-in show for teenagers on the subject of sex. We met him at his campus office and expressed our concern over our daughter's decision to become sexually active and our confusion about it. Here's how our conversation developed, along with thoughts we later shared with each other:

DR. DAILEY: Were you surprised to learn your daughter was having sex?

US: Yes, we—

DR. DAILEY: *Really?* With our daughters we anticipated it. We expected it.

US: (*How do you respond to a statement like that? And why would he tell us that?*) Well, you're not the average parent, so maybe it was easier for you. We thought we'd raised our daughters to behave differently. We were stunned when we learned that she's been doing so many things counter to the message we delivered to her—

DR. DAILEY: That you *thought* you had delivered to her. Your underlying message was, "Here's a little bit about sex, but don't do it." I'd guess you're like most parents. Maybe you didn't teach your kids that the stork brought them, but you also weren't open about sexuality.

US: (*Now how would you know what we . . .*) Well, we tried to—that is, we . . .

DR. DAILEY: The message my wife and I gave to our daughters was, "Here's a *lot* about sex. When you do it, we hope it's really, really good for you. Why don't you learn how to have an orgasm so you can enjoy it? *Learn* something about your body!"

US: (*He talked to his daughters about orgasm? Parents don't do that!*) Hmmm. That's, ah, well, an *interesting* approach.

DR. DAILEY: Did you give your daughters sex education?

US: Oh yes. (*At last! A question we can actually answer!*) An excellent course that taught—

DR. DAILEY: Plumbing, right? I know all about those courses. They teach physiology and anatomy, contraception and sexually transmitted diseases, and *not once* is anything mentioned about intimacy, orgasm, and sexual closeness. Your underlying message to your daughters has been, "Wait. Don't do it. *Do not.* Keep your zipper up. Save it for marriage. Learn about sex, but don't be sexual."

US: *(We didn't actually expect them to wait until marriage. We did hope they would wait.)* Well, we—

DR. DAILEY: I'll bet you've delivered all those unspoken messages, as most parents have. Every family has unspoken rules and every member of the family knows them. When I was in family-therapy training, one of my most remarkable discoveries was the meta-communication insanity that I had grown up with—the underlying communication that can include facial expressions, removing certain books, deflecting from certain topics, making comments in front of teenagers when things happen on television shows—all of that.

US: *(It's hard talking to someone who interrupts all the time.)* But you have to keep them from—

DR. DAILEY: No. *You can't!* We are sexual human beings from the moment we are born until we die. You have *no choice* as to whether your daughters are or aren't sexual, because they were born sexual and they'll die sexual. Just like you. My guess is that neither of you, on the occasion of your first sexual intercourse, thinking that the day had arrived, phoned your mom to say, "Mom, I'm not sure, but I think I'm gonna get laid tonight and I just want to check on how you feel about it." My guess is that you did not ask permission. You were sexual and you did it.

As parents, you have no choice and very little influence over whether your children will express their sexuality. The only influence you have is on *what* they will bring to that experience. That's *it*. If you start with that assumption, you raise children very differently.

US: *(He's got to be kidding!)* You mean, with your daughters—

DR. DAILEY: When they were born, my wife and I told each other that we were raising somebody's lovers. You look shocked. *(Yes, we were.)* But what we had decided was that when they chose to express their sexuality, as we knew they would someday, we wanted it to be *really* good for them. We didn't want them to be part of the 90 percent of women who, on the occasion of their first sexual intercourse, respond with, "Is that it?" We wanted them to have a sexual experience that would *knock their socks off!*

We were also very clear with them from the time they became interested in boys that if you date an asshole, you marry an asshole. If you date an alcoholic, you get an alcoholic. If you date somebody who beats you up, you're going to marry somebody who beats you up. You get what you see. It's your choice. We can't save you.

A lot of women have these romantic notions that if they love a man more, care for him more, that somehow he'll shape up. That's not how it goes. They have to understand that.

US: *(Now he's starting to make a lot of sense!)* Yes, that's important. We think our daughter's boyfriend is awful. It's not just the sex. In so many ways he's had a negative influence on her.

DR. DAILEY: But she responds to something in him. For you to regard him as a loser, as you clearly do, isn't fair because you're devaluing her choice, in part because she chose to have sex with him.

US: *(Wait a minute, he's taking her side. He doesn't know the Boyfriend.)* But she's so young.

DR. DAILEY: So what you're saying is that your daughter is not supposed to be sexual until a certain age, at which time she can be sexual. That's what you're saying. That doesn't make any sense to me. Teenagers *are sexual.* They have sexual feelings. They have sexual fantasies. Their eroticism is alive in them, just like intellect, spirituality, and emotion are alive in them. It's there.

When a young girl of thirteen feels a rush of eroticism, and at the same time she's hearing all kinds of messages about virginity and save it and you're not supposed to be sexual yet, that's real confusing, especially if nobody has affirmed the erotic within her. It makes her crazy. That's why a lot of teenagers feel like they're nuts!

I ask my students how many of them had a class in school on orgasms and how you have the damn things. Nobody ever raises their hand. And we wonder in this society why there are so many non-orgasmic females who fake orgasm their entire marriages! My students are embarrassed by that topic, but they want openness and honesty. They *want* that.

I know some sixteen-year-olds who are more ready to have sexual intercourse than some thirty-year-olds. It's not something that's age variable. Not by a long shot.

US: *(Not to say orgasm isn't nice, but as a topic of discussion with a sixteen-year-old?)* But our sixteen-year-old daughter is too young to—

DR. DAILEY: Wait a minute, *wait* a minute. See, that's the kind of thinking that makes teenagers *crazy*. Because what you're saying is that teenagers are not supposed to be sexual until a certain age, at which time they can now be sexual. That doesn't make any sense because *everyone* is born sexual. They have sexual feelings, sexual fantasies. It's *there*. What you mean is that you'd like for your daughter to not *have sex* until she's older, but that's *not* your choice.

US: *(Whoa! Now you wait a minute!)* But early sex can—

DR. DAILEY: *Listen* to yourself! When you refer to sex, what do you mean? We are *all* sexual. You're referring to *early sexual intercourse.* Not early oral sex, not early breast fondling, not early deep kissing or petting, not early fantasizing. You have *got to hear what you're saying!*

US: *(This is off the wall!)* Are *you* saying that if sixteen-year-olds feel ready, they should go ahead and engage in intercourse?

DR. DAILEY: Absolutely!

US: *(We're getting a little nervous here.)* Should a thirteen-year-old?

DR. DAILEY: *Absolutely!*

US: *(What will he say next?)* Don't parents get rather *upset* when you say this?

DR. DAILEY: Yes! They say, "Wait a minute, what are you talking about!" But I don't tell them what I just told you. I don't say that thirteen-year-olds and sixteen-year-olds might be ready for sex. They need to realize that on their own. Instead I say, "Let's find out how the consequences of your sexual upbringing are now playing themselves out in your sexual relationship." To understand their own children, which they must do if they're going to have honest communication with them, I believe parents must recall those sexual feelings and needs they had when they were young, and the *anger* they experienced because they didn't get sex education and because there's such a double standard in our society. Women need to get furious that there's more talk in our society about female virgins than male virgins.

So I invite these parents back to their own adolescence, into their own history. If I can successfully take them back, after that they don't get quite as uppity and quite as judgmental about their teenagers.

US: *(Hmmm. That is an interesting idea. Let's hear a little more.)* And how do you get them to go back?

DR. DAILEY: Remind them of what it was like to be six and out in the barn with their cousins playing peekaboo and touching each other's genitals and noticing erections. How in junior high if you were a boy you lied about having done it when you hadn't yet. What it was like at age sixteen to be with your date in the back seat of a '55 Chevy and what a mystery it all was and how exciting it all was. I ask them if they would really want to take all that back and if they would want to take it away from their own children.

If parents were more in touch with their own sexuality, they would be in a better position to be there for their kids or their mate. I can teach women about the concept of orgasm in forty-five seconds, but it takes me hours to talk about what the barriers are. I can define premature ejaculation as the primary male dysfunction in our society in four seconds, but *why* is it that so many men suffer from it? What is the pressure, the fear of failure, the physiological anxiety that triggers that response? What it comes down to is, can you become a different kind of lover? Not someone who leaps tall buildings, but *someone who is there in the moment.* And boy, that's real different for a lot of men.

US: *(Okay, that makes sense.)* But to help children get in touch with their sexuality—

DR. DAILEY: You have to give them the information they need. Right now what most kids hear is taught in courses called something like "health"—which seems to imply that sexuality is a disease. It is *not a disease.* Sexuality does not necessarily mean intercourse. Too many people think that. In fact, you two are perfect examples of it. Sex education tries to scare people out of having sex, and it doesn't work.

The research on children raised in fundamental evangelical homes is really interesting because it shows that their incidence of sexual intercourse is exactly the same as that of other children. But they get pregnant more often. Why? Because they *don't anticipate being sexual.* They don't talk about it.

You want to know how to keep a twelve-year-old from having sex? Put a chastity belt on her. Or create so much guilt, so much shame, that any sexual experience she has is so aversive to her that she becomes phobic and will never be able to enjoy sex. Then you will have created my private practice patient load.

Did you know that 50 percent of all couples have serious sexual dysfunction sometime in their relationships? Why is that?

US: *(Hey, we aren't the experts here.)* Well . . .

DR. DAILEY: Because adolescence is a breeding ground for sexual dysfunction. People believe you can put all that guilt and shame on somebody, and then, when they get married, everything will be fine. No! They will carry the guilt and shame for the rest of their lives.

You know why parents get so uptight about their kids' sexuality? Because their kids are living their parents' lives, repeating what they did.

US: *(At least this time he answered his own question.)* That happens to every generation.

DR. DAILEY: Exactly. Why are some fathers so concerned that their daughters might get raped? Because the fathers coerced women to get sex on dates and are themselves in that respect rapists.

AIDS gives adults another way to control teenagers. We control instead of teaching our children that sexuality is a natural, normal part of the human condition. Why is our Western society so uptight about sexuality compared with other cultures? Why are places like Sweden so different from us?

US: *(Why is that?)* Yes, why is that?

DR. DAILEY: Attitude. We're not comfortable with sexuality in this culture. If, for example, you genuinely affirmed your children's sexuality from birth, then at age three when you found them playing diddly-diddly with their cousins, instead of going crazy, you'd go, "There it is, there's that erotic stuff right there and I'd better get out of here so they can enjoy themselves. I don't want to interrupt that, because it's glorious and so special."

I think if somebody invented an implant that could be placed in newborn infants that could guarantee they would not feel lust or have sexual intercourse before the age of twenty, massive numbers of parents would get them for their kids. We tell our kids, "If you do it, you'll get pregnant! You'll get cankers on your ding-dong and it'll fall off!" Well, that isn't going to keep teenagers from having sexual intercourse.

We live in a society where there is a strong reproductive bias. We teach that the only good sex is sex that could result in a socially sanctioned and approved pregnancy. All other sex is wrong.

US: *(What he's saying is making a lot of sense.)* Yet the message coming through the media is all about sex.

DR. DAILEY: Welcome to Western civilized culture!

US: *(Now we're getting the hang of this.)* Society is saying, "Do it, do it, do it."

DR. DAILEY: No, society is saying, "Sexual stuff, particularly woman sexual stuff, sells things." It doesn't have anything to do with "go out and have sexual intercourse." What teenagers see on television or at the movies doesn't influence their behavior. If that were true, then all the messages from parents and the church and society about "Don't do it" and the fact that there was *no* sex education not too many years ago would have kept kids from having sex, and the fact is, they were out there bopping each other regularly.

US: *(We can't accept that as correct. All that sex in the media has got to have a strong influence.)* So you're saying that neither one works.

DR. DAILEY: Right! *Neither one works!* Because neither one affirms the reality that kids are sexual human beings and in spite of anything they see in the media they will at some point in their lives elect to share that part of themselves with someone else.

The few kids who actually get sexuality education in which they have the opportunity to explore feelings and attitudes as well as facts will, according to research, delay their first sexual intercourse experience—not a whole lot, but some—and their incidence of pregnancy and sexually transmitted diseases will be dramatically lower. Why? Because these kids *anticipate* that they're going to be sexual. They prepare for that part of their lives.

We must help our children affirm their sexuality and help them make choices that have positive outcomes. We must invite them, in a nonrepressive way, into the reality of their sexuality. That's a *sex-positive* stand, as opposed to a sex-negative stand.

US: *(This is overwhelming. We'll have to sort it through later.)* How can parents who want their children to have positive outcomes with their sexuality, but who didn't experience this themselves and who are not experts on it, help their children with this?

DR. DAILEY: Don't lie. Give them straight stuff. If you're embarrassed when you talk about it, your kids pick up both the words and the embarrassment—and hang on to the embarrassment.

US: *(But it is embarrassing.)* Can you say, "This makes me a little nervous, but I'm going to try—"

DR. DAILEY: Of course! The parent can say, "This really makes me uncomfortable, and it's not so much because of my relationship with you but because of my own upbringing. I'd like to share a little bit with you about what that was like." At the same time you say, "I know what the realities are."

Feeling uncomfortable is no problem. What drives teenagers nuts is parents' *pretending* to know it all, or giving only half an answer. If you're not ready to answer honestly when your kid says, "Dad, did you have sex as a teenager?," then you're not ready for this. But if you can do it, if you can prepare them for this part of their lives, then they won't end up at sixteen in the back of an automobile having their first act of sexual intercourse when the condoms are in the drugstore. The condoms are in their pocket because they *know* there's a very good possibility that they will elect to have sex sometime in the near future. They don't always know with whom, why, or where, but they do know it and they are affirmed of that knowledge. So they are prepared because they have been taught that they are sexual human beings. *Both* the boys *and* the girls have been taught this.

We gave our daughters condoms when they started their periods, because, as we told them, we knew that at some point they would engage in sexual intercourse and we wanted them to be safe.

It should be a goal for parents that their children's sexual experiences bring them the richest affirmation of self and the fullest pleasure. US: *(You gave your daughters* condoms? *Weren't they embarrassed?)* But most parents also feel strongly that engaging in sexual intercourse is not appropriate for teenagers. You said a while ago that you believed engaging in sex was okay for the thirteen-year-old who felt ready for it. Most parents just can't accept that.

DR. DAILEY: But they also can't prevent it.

US: (*Surely they can do* <u>*something!*</u>) Well, can they at least influence their children to wait until they're older?

DR. DAILEY: Age is no guarantee of anything. But you can tell them that "getting pregnant and having children when you can take care of them is probably better, so when you have sexual intercourse, there are some variables you might want to take into consideration." And then you teach them responsible birth control.

Kids today know *facts*. That's not the issue. Knowing about AIDS doesn't prevent AIDS. Knowing how to use a condom prevents AIDS. If a kid says, "I don't know how to put on a condom," then demonstrate how to put a condom on a banana. Most kids have never actually held a condom and may use it wrong when the time comes, or can't get it on at all, or tear the package so the condom stretches or gets holes in it. Help them practice. A girl may ask if using a condom will diminish a male's sexual pleasure—an argument guys like to give girls—and you can tell her that with a good condom he'll lose about 10 percent of the sensation, but if that 10 percent is so important that he wants to risk pregnancy, then maybe he's not the right partner for her. And don't just tell them to use a spermicide, buy it for them and explain how it's used so they'll know how when the time comes, because they won't take time then to read the instructions. And *don't* shy away from their questions. Of course, it means that you as parents must be educated about sex.

As for the rest of it, we told our daughters that we wanted them to enjoy their first sexual experience. We said, "We hope it's consensual. Above all, we hope you don't get raped. You can learn some things about drinking that will help lessen your chances of getting into that situation. We don't want you to have an experience that leaves you saying, "That was it?" We want you to be able to tell your partner exactly what you want and need, so you must figure out what you want and need before you do it."

We wanted our daughters to express their sexuality over their lifetimes with curiosity, with fantasy, with all kinds of sex.

US: *(But what teen wants parents that involved in their sex life?)* But many parents are afraid if they do this, if they give their children these messages, they'll encourage their children to be sexually active.

DR. DAILEY: Remember: They're going to do that anyway. You *won't* influence that decision, only whether it's a good experience or a bad one. It's the same with their values. Parents say, "We want our kids to have our values." We didn't do that with our kids. We said, "Here are our values. Here are values very different from ours. Those values held by others have as much credence as ours. We made choices and we live with them, even if they cost us. We want you to know the range of value options. To the extent you choose our values, so be it. Your business is to create your own value structure."

US: *(This is radical. Can you be a college professor in the middle of Kansas and say these things?)* If parents accept that they can only influence but cannot control their children's decisions or values, what can they do if they have no history of affirming their children's sexuality? What if in the past the parents have given out all the wrong messages?

DR. DAILEY: If parents sincerely want to try to undo some of the harm, they must begin by apologizing to their children. Tell them you've blown it and you're very sorry, that you were embarrassed and scared and a lot of it had to do with how you were brought up.

If your apology is genuine, they'll be angry at first, because of the way you acted in the past, but they'll come around. The parent-child relationship is unbelievably sustaining.

But if your apology is not genuine, your kids will know it and they'll blow it off.

You know, it's a little ironic that two people like you would be surprised that your sixteen-year-old was having sex. See, *I'm* surprised that *you're* surprised, because my reaction was, "Of course! Of course she's having sex!"

US: *(That's not fair. We didn't raise her to— Wait a minute. Maybe he's right. It was her decision and we didn't influence it. We just* _thought_ *we did.)* We're starting to understand that we haven't really talked to our daughters about sexuality, about their personal needs and feelings. We've got to learn how to.

DR. DAILEY: I'd say only 2 to 4 percent of parents do a good job with sex education and sexuality education. But there aren't enough well-trained sex educators to do it, so parents must try. The embarrassment you feel over doing it is an embarrassment that arises out of having not done these things for sixteen years. We celebrated our daughters' menstruation with them. They weren't embarrassed because we didn't start sex education with them the day they menstruated. We'd been talking about that for years. Parents can't go home and lay sex education on their kids because they're gonna tune you out, or else they're gonna say, "Why didn't you tell me that before?" They can get very angry about it. I would say to your daughter, "So you're having sexual intercourse. Are you having orgasms? If you're going to have sex, let's make it good."

US: *(Parents actually talk to their kids like that?)* We're not sure we could talk to our daughter about orgasm.

DR. DAILEY: Then find another way to get the information to her. Give her a book, get her in the right class, not just a class on plumbing. Help her to become a sexually happy adult. You've got to remember that your daughter isn't having sex to upset you. She's out there seeking some way to find affirmation.

US: *(Okay, okay, we agree on that point.)* You've certainly given us some things to think about—

DR. DAILEY: If you want to do this right, if you want to open up true dialogue and discussion with your daughters, you need to know yourselves better. You must know where you're coming from and why. If you can help yourselves, you'll then be able to help your children. And to do that, you've got to start by knowing your own story. You've got to be able to tell that story, because that's all you've got. You must do this because you are sexual human beings and you're trying to get a little smarter about it. You need to work through your personal issues, and exploring your own personal story may influence where you go.

US: *(That sounds painful, tedious, and time-consuming. We have careers to pursue.)* Oh, that's so long ago. We'd never remember things that happened twenty to thirty years ago.

DR. DAILEY: It will start to come back to you. It will help you understand where your daughters are today. If you're sincere about wanting to establish strong communication with your daughters on the subject of sexuality, you've got to do this. You must tell your story.

CHAPTER 5

DAYS OF
FUTURE PASSED

By confronting our narrow way of thinking, Dr. Dailey forced us to think about teens and sex very differently than we had before. After our visit with him, we found ourselves first rejecting and then eventually accepting almost everything he had said to us. We still weren't sure that some thirteen-year-olds were ready for sex—that seemed extreme—nor were we convinced that teens' sexual behavior wasn't influenced by the media's message of "Do it, do it, do it."

We did agree, however, that whether or not teenagers got the message from the media to do or not to do it, many of them will do it anyway.

He had told us we needed to learn more about ourselves and our own sexuality. His challenge to us to tell our own stories weighed heavily on us. How could we do that? Neither of us could remember much—a fact, a name, an event here and there, but there was no *story* to be told. Nothing in our own histories seemed at all remarkable or interesting.

That was an excuse, because we knew that wasn't his point. Dr. Dailey had said remembering our personal stories would help us know ourselves better and allow us in turn to understand our daughters better and be able to assist them in the difficult task of growing up. We really wanted that. It made sense to us that if we were more in touch with our own sexuality at the ages our daughters now were, we would be more comfortable with *their* sexuality.

It meant exposing more about ourselves than we were sure we wanted to, but after some discussion, we decided to take the risk. By discovering through remembrance our personal histories, we could show other parents what to think about if they decided to "go back." Perhaps, depending on the old selves we found in our pasts, we could share with our daughters the startling fact that even though we might seem like fossils to them, we *were* once young, and maybe we were even a little bit like them.

With foggy memories and no idea where it would all go, we each put pen to paper. It took a number of tries for both of us. With each attempt we remembered more, until finally our stories took shape.

Andrea Goes First

When I turned sixteen in October 1962, I had one goal above all others: escape from my hometown.

Newman Grove, Nebraska, population 1,000, was a good place to grow up, but I was convinced that if I had to live there the rest of my life I would die of boredom. In the one-room library tucked away in the Odd Fellows Hall, I had read every book I was allowed to check out by the time I started high school in the ninth grade, and I *knew* a lot of world was waiting out there. I wasn't going to do anything to endanger my chances of seeing and experiencing it.

Like falling in love with a hometown boy. That was a struggle for me, because I started falling in love when I was quite young, first with my favorite actors and singers, and then with local high school athletes. Sometimes my feelings were so intense they scared me. As young as sixth grade I'd go to football and basketball games, even though I didn't much like sports, just to stare at the current object of my desire. And I always had crushes on my older brother's friends. When they were in our home, I would get scattered and tongue-tied.

But by the time I was in ninth grade I was working hard to contain these feelings, because I'd heard too many Newman Grove stories about married folks who had started dating in junior or senior high school and were now celebrating their fiftieth wedding anniversaries. I might fantasize about my latest love interest when I lay in bed at night, but my intention was to keep Newman Grove boys at arm's length.

My resolve didn't last, of course. Growing up involves lots of age-appropriate markers in little Midwest towns. In Newman Grove you could start dating, in cars, in the ninth grade. I didn't want to miss the fun, and from the beginning of ninth grade on I dated— but on my terms.

The fifties and the early sixties were a quiet, peaceful time in my corner of the world. The thrifty Scandinavians who populated Newman Grove and the surrounding area worked hard. It seemed to me that most of them were named Johnson, Nelson, Larson, Olson, or Hansen. They were honest, religious, reliable, Lutheran, and dull. My family were outsiders. My parents, both of British and Irish descent, and my brother moved to Newman Grove before I was born. I was followed some years later by my younger brother and two younger sisters.

Dad started out as the high school coach and eventually became superintendent of schools, a position that elevated the five of us to the unenviable position of having to behave as good as preachers' kids. I hated being told by my mother that I had to set a good example, and by my friends and detractors that anything I got, whether it was a good grade or the lead in the class play, was because my old man was the super and the teachers were afraid of me. That was another reason to escape—I wanted to be *me* and not the superintendent's kid.

Another was that as eldest daughter I was expected to be junior mother and assistant housekeeper. I often resented the limitations this created on my life.

I had no interest in emulating my mother's life, though it had some pluses. She and her friends would get together for coffee at least one morning a week, play bridge together twice a month, and host family picnics and get-togethers. Only a few women worked outside the home. All the women were active in the local churches and attended all the school activities and community organizations. Husbands walked home at noon for lunch. The whole town would turn out for a funeral, a parade, and the high school Christmas program. Life was sweet.

But I didn't want it, so my dilemma was how to have a boyfriend without getting serious about him. Sixteen was an especially critical time for me because many of my girlfriends were already settling in with boyfriends they would eventually marry. I wanted to marry someday, but having children seemed too intangible to imagine.

"Going all the way," as we referred to it, interested me a lot and marriage, as I knew very well, was the only way that would be permissible. In those times and in that place, you were either a good girl or a bad girl—one who did it or one who waited. My girlfriends and I had been raised to believe that to be a virgin on our wedding nights would be to give our husbands the ultimate gift.

I can't say that at sixteen I knew very much about sex. Certainly I knew far less than my daughters at sixteen. You took your clothes off and he put his thing in you, and that was about it. It

sounded pretty revolting. I didn't concentrate much on the act itself. What interested me was the sensualism of being naked with
someone. *That* interested me. Sleeping in the same bed with
someone and having easy access to them interested me too.

There was a gang of us, both boys and girls, who were together
through grade school and junior high. As we started to mature, our
play life together changed. We all rode our bicycles to and from
school, and by fifth grade the boys would chase us girls home from
school, spinning their bikes around us and calling us names and
laughing at us. It was paramount that we girls always be in clusters
and never be caught alone by them, so we accompanied each other
home in meticulously executed arrangements that left no one with
more than a half block to be by herself. We were rarely assaulted
on our own blocks, for the neighbors would report the boys to their
fathers if they teased us too much. Of course, we secretly liked the
teasing, but we pretended to hate the boys and spent considerable
energies telling them so.

My most serious crush—an on-again, off-again one that lasted
for years—was on a boy named Larry. He was cute, red-haired and
freckled, personable, and a born tease who was always into mis-
chief. I would pretend to his face that I disliked him, but he would
be the one whose attention I wanted and who I would have to confess to liking when my girlfriends and I played truth-telling games.
He was the first boy I slow-danced with and the first boy I kissed,
though we never dated. Larry's role in my life was to make me
appreciate that I was a girl. We stayed good friends all through
high school.

I always had a rich fantasy life and I remember that in seventh
and eighth grade I would have these running stories in my head as
I went about my daily existence. A favorite movie star—Bobby
Darin or Brandon de Wilde—would be by my side while I practiced my piano lesson or when I babysat the neighbors' children or

helped my sisters get ready for bed. We would have imaginary conversations and I would nuzzle a pillow, pretending it was my latest
paramour's cheek, or snuggle into my pillows at night, pressing my
body into his. My fantasies were fairly tame, but I didn't know
that, and they were always a source of some kind of vague guilt
for me.

I grew up sexually naive. My parents were protective enough
and I was lucky enough that I was never sexually abused, nor did I
ever see anything I shouldn't have, nor did I hear about sexual de-
viancy. I didn't even know what homosexuality was until I started
college. Scandal rarely tainted that innocent time. The Cold War
going on out there in the big wide world barely touched us. Eisen-
hower, a Midwesterner, was in the White House. We considered
him family. Since Kennedy was a Democrat, an Easterner, and,
worst of all, a Catholic, he was only grudgingly admired in Newman Grove, though all of us thought Jackie was just wonderful and
that she and Jack were the perfect couple. Through it all I was
safe, and that was good, but I was also so innocent that I might not
have known danger had it threatened me.

Or a friend. I remember a girlfriend telling me about something her big brother occasionally did to her that she didn't dare
tell her mother about. He would come into her room when their
parents were gone and he was babysitting with her and he would
pull down his pants and make her pull down hers and then he
would get on top of her and this white stuff would come out of
him and get on her stomach. I had no idea what she was talking
about—my older brother paid no attention to me whatsoever—and
it didn't occur to me that I should tell my mother about it.

Or if it had occurred to me, I might not have told her anyway—not only because I didn't know that what my friend's brother
was doing was wrong, but also because I was far too embarrassed to
talk to my mother about anything that had to do with my body.

The messages sent to me about my femininity were mixed. I didn't glory in being female. My parents didn't give me that. Eventually the boys and men in my life with whom I would be romantically and/or sexually associated would have to give me that. No, the messages I grew up with from my family and my community were to be modest and virtuous, to marry and have babies. I don't remember my parents ever talking to me about sex or love or feelings. In fact, when my period started, my mother had never talked to me about what a period was and that I would be getting one. I knew what was happening to me only because a friend of mine had started hers and she had older sisters and had shared some information with me. But when mine started the summer before my thirteenth birthday, I was so embarrassed I hid my bloody panties. When my mother found them, *then* she told me what was happening to me and she gave me a box of big thick sanitary napkins and one of those torturous elastic belts that were supposed to keep them in place (but didn't do a very good job of it) and a booklet called *Now That You're a Woman* that spoke in wondrous terms about "role" and "duty" and "womanhood" and made it sound like all the fun was over and the hard work was beginning.

She also told my father, and I remember him teasing me about my period starting. I was so horrified at him having this knowledge of me that it was all I could do after that to look him in the eye. He made me feel like he knew something about me that I didn't know about myself—some secret knowledge about the sexual part of me. It was uncomfortable and disturbing and it made relations difficult between us for years, because I had to pretend that I wasn't those things he knew I was and that I had no interest in sex.

Yet it was my father who provided the only sex education I received. Like most people in Newman Grove, Dad didn't think kindly of Catholics, whom he referred to as rednecks or pope lovers. When I was a freshman in high school I dated a Catholic boy

I liked very much. He was nice, polite, smart, and lots of fun. But he came from a large Catholic farm family. My father liked him but didn't want me dating him—he said, "You'll marry him and then you'll whelp every year"—even though I was only fourteen. Dad's rare references to sex were usually in such barnyard terms, often with a smirk on his face. Dutiful daughter that I was, I did stop dating my Catholic boyfriend. Having my father hassle me about it at home just wasn't worth it. A year later the boy was killed in an accident and I truly grieved for him and hoped his Catholic God would take him straight to heaven.

My girlfriends and I were quite modest with one another once our bodies started to develop. We didn't have gym classes, so there were no group showers to help us get through that. Our clothing was also modest. The dress code imposed on us by our families, the school, and the community would allow nothing else. I grew up wearing saddle shoes, bulky socks, circle skirts, and cardigan sweaters over white blouses. Naturally, I had a ponytail. We girls learned to keep our knees together, because there were always a few boys who would try to see up our skirts. We were both re-pulsed and titillated by this, but we only acted repulsed.

We were all very interested in who was going with whom at the high school, and we studied each couple whenever we had the op-portunity. On prom night we sat on the steps to the gym watching the couples come and go, commenting on each girl's dress and hairstyle.

When I was in eighth grade, the older sister of one of my best friends ran off with her boyfriend and got married. General specu-lation was that a baby was on the way, but it turned out one wasn't. They just wanted to be married. They had been one of those couples tenderly and devotedly in love forever. She was very pretty and a cheerleader and he was very handsome and a sports star, and we girls thought it was all terribly romantic, scandalous though it was and disapproving though our elders were, and embarrassed though my friend and her family were.

Today they wouldn't have had to get married in order to have sex, but back then there was no other way. Guys had no way to get condoms. The birth-control pill wasn't yet around, although it was about to be. And anyway, even if you wanted to do it, you had been told so much that it was wrong that you sort of halfway believed it. Your status went from virgin to whore in a single moment. Up the street from us in a sorry little house lived a young couple who had "had" to get married. They were Catholic and they had several little children. She always looked thin and pale and tired, and her husband had to work a couple of jobs, and perhaps it's just my imagination that my mother's nose was slightly in the air when we passed their house, but the message out there in the airwaves was that if you had sex while you were a teenager, *that would be you! Your life would be ruined!*

So instead we just smoldered. In seventh and eighth grades my friends and I would have boy-girl class parties at one another's homes, usually in a basement rec room, that were fraught with sexual tension created by overheated, maturing young bodies. Mostly we would stand around in groups, the girls giggling and gossiping, the boys acting silly. We ate cupcakes and ham salad sandwiches and drank punch and tried not to sweat. There was always a record player and we would pool our records, jitterbugging to the Big Bopper or the Everly Brothers. When Ricky Nelson's "Lonesome Town" or Elvis's "Love Me Tender" was played, we'd quickly pair up. If parents were out of the room (some were more discreet than others), someone always switched off the lights for a moment or two and we'd dance a little closer, then pull back in embarrassment, surprised at the responses of our bodies, which begged for more.

Aside from a couple of quick kisses with Larry in junior high, my first real kiss was shortly after I started ninth grade and I began going with Richard, a tenth-grader who was very good-looking and very nice but not real bright. Richard was sort of shy and not much of a conversationalist. I liked him in a shivers-down-the-spine sort of way because of his looks. There was this huge buildup to that first kiss. We went to several school functions and to several movies together first, and we would hold hands. Nice girls didn't give good-night kisses before the third date, and nice boys didn't expect them to. Both of us knew that. Finally, one evening when he had walked me up to the door (we had gone out at least five or six times), it happened. I had practiced and practiced, of course, but the real thing didn't feel like much. More like two noses touching. I had been expecting magic.

Richard and I kissed several more times after that but it never got better. That's when I moved on to my Catholic boyfriend, who was much more experienced than Richard and who kissed me hard on the third date. I liked it so much I kissed back. I had thought kissing was supposed to be a rather chaste activity. The movies I'd been allowed to see certainly made it seem so. It was something of a relief to break up with him because of this disturbing physical attraction I felt for him—plus my fears that I would never get out of Newman Grove. He was very nice about my father's objections to his Catholicism and immediately started going out with another Protestant girl whose family probably also objected to his religion.

There were other boyfriends, other kisses that freshman year. There was even some parking in dark cars on country roads and some light petting. I didn't cross any boundaries I knew I shouldn't.

When I was fifteen and a sophomore, I had my first serious boyfriend. He was a senior, popular, a scholar and an athlete, and getting him to ask me out became a challenge for me. I was thrilled when he did. I liked him a lot, and for the first time I settled into a relationship with someone for longer than just a few dates. I was beyond the experimenting-with-kissing stage, or just seeing what it was like to park with a guy and get all goose-pimply wondering what would happen next. But there was that old problem of his being from Newman Grove.

So even when I was dating him I was pushing him away. It was very confusing. I still have vivid memories of the first time we parked on a country road overlooking town. It was a starry night and the lights from town twinkled below us. The world was completely silent after he turned off the car engine. We sat there, he behind the steering wheel and me in the middle of the seat nestled close to him. And then he turned to me and I was waiting demurely but expectantly, and finally, hesitantly, he kissed me, wrapping his arms around me. And for the first time I was freely kissing back and I liked how he smelled (English Leather) and how strong his muscular arms were when they went around me and how we kind of blended into each other.

My body was just full of tingles and meltdowns and yearnings. But all the time we parked we both knew what the boundaries were and respected them. And when we would finally pull back from each other, we were both fuzzy with desire and urges and trying to keep our hands in the right places, and then we would kiss again and finally make ourselves stop, and then he would start the car and we would drive slowly and silently into town, holding hands, content to be together but crazy with frustration from our bodies' unfulfilled sexual yearnings.

Eventually I lost interest in him and suggested he ask out one of my friends who liked him. He did and they really hit it off. If you want to know the end of the story, eventually they got married, had children—and didn't live in Newman Grove.

As my junior year of high school started, I was more determined than ever that once out of high school I would move away

forever. Knowing that education was the key and I was going to
need a college scholarship, I buckled down to my studies. I wanted
to go to Girls State the following summer, and since I was the superintendent's daughter, I had to be better than anyone else to be
considered, or, if selected, it would look like favoritism. I had a
full load of studies and activities and a part-time job, plus all my
responsibilities at home. But I was sixteen and I also wanted to be
part of all the social activities. I needed a boyfriend of
convenience.

My victim was a sweet guy in my geometry class who had become my buddy. I knew he liked me but was afraid to ask me out.
Maybe I finally asked him, or maybe I put my friends up to getting
him to ask me, but finally the task was accomplished and we became an item. He never got to first base with me—simple good-
night kisses were the limit. I was in full control of my emotions at
all times. And that's how I spent my junior year of high school. I
was busy morning, noon, and night with all my responsibilities,
and when I needed help with math or when there was a social
event, I had my sweet boyfriend. I'm sure it was a far more fulfilling situation for me than it was for him, but I was indifferent to
that. I was restless, anxious to grow up, eager to be independent
and away from home.

I had little true communication with my parents. My mother's
concern was that I get good grades, be in lots of activities, hold a
part-time job, and still help out as much as possible at home. I
tried hard not to be home. The only refuge I had there was my
own bedroom, provided I could keep my younger siblings *out*. I
rarely saw my older brother. My younger brother was a terrible
tease who loved to spy on me and I considered him a nuisance.
My little sisters needed me more than I realized. My only relationship to them was having to take care of them, so I certainly didn't
appreciate them. I had no intimate conversations with my parents.

I never felt I could do enough to please them. No matter how good my grades were or what honors I might have garnered, I never had the impression it was good enough. It seems to me that I always sought the approval of the other adults around me. I wanted them to like me. Scandinavians rarely give praise, so verbal reinforcement from other adults that I was doing okay was tough to come by. Fortunately, there were a few who offered it, and while my self-esteem often suffered and has held me back on many occasions, I also had enough determination to figure out how to get what I wanted.

That summer of 1963, when I was sixteen and between my junior and senior years of high school, I managed to get out of town for three months—my first time away from home. I only got as far as my grandparents' home in Hastings, which was two hours from Newman Grove, but it was a start. I had applied for a summer student internship at the regional state hospital there because at the time I had some interest in psychology. When I got it, I somehow managed to get both my parents and my grandparents to agree to my summer move. My mother was concerned at the loss of my help at home, but I was determined to do this, and my grandparents were willing.

I loved being free of all the responsibilities of home, and I felt very grown up. I was very fond of my grandmother. She kept a careful eye on me, but she also loved to spoil me. For my part, being an only child and living in a quiet, orderly household with no small children, if only temporarily, was a heady experience.

I began working at my new job, going through locked doors each day to assist in an occupational-therapy program for mental patients. I found it thrilling. All that boredom for all those years in tiny Newman Grove, and now I was doing something *important*. Then I went to Girls State for a week, and when I got back I met Rick.

That was it for me. From the time I first met him, I was
wildly, desperately, passionately, romantically in love. My feelings
ran amok, different from anything I'd ever known before. Before
I'd always been able to rein in, control my feelings and the situation. But not now. I truly felt I had no will of my own and that I
would love him forever. He was a year older than I and getting
ready to go off to the state university. He was smart and polite and
very verbal and funny and ambitious. That he was interested in me
seemed like a miracle.

We didn't need a destination when we were together that summer, although we were usually doing something. We just needed
to be in each other's presence to be happy. We could take a walk
in the summer night heat as fireflies flitted around us, sit on my
grandparents' big porch, take a drive in his '55 Ford, watch a ball
game, or go to a movie. It didn't matter. Being together mattered.
Touching each other, looking into each other's eyes, making each
other laugh—that's what mattered. Rick had been raised in a home
similar enough to mine that we had the same values, the same
morals, the same censures on us. But we loved each other and we
wanted each other, and we went as far as we could without breaking the rules. Our kisses were deep and promising, our hands urgent on each other. When I would come home from being out
with him I would be in a state of agitation for what seemed like
hours, so stimulated was my body.

We both had curfews, but as soon as he got home after kissing
me good night at my grandparents' door, he would call me and we
would each sit in the dark in our respective houses and talk as long
as we could. My grandparents went to bed early and slept soundly,
so I didn't disturb them as I sat in the hallway by the kitchen, talking on their one black telephone. Sometimes Rick's parents would
give him an ultimatum and we would have to hang up, which was
just as well, since we both had jobs to go to the next day, but I can

still recall those long middle-of-the-night conversations and how the next day I would go over everything we had said to each other and savor anything endearing he had said to me. It didn't take us long to begin saying "I love you"—the first time I'd ever said that to anyone—or to begin hinting at a future together.

When it was time for me to return home for my senior year of high school and for Rick to go off to the university, he gave me his class ring and I wore it the whole next year, wrapping it with tape until it bulged, a symbol to all that I was his.

I think I knew when I was leaving Hastings that I had just experienced the most special summer of my life. I was sixteen and love would never again be so achingly sweet, lust so tortured, or sex so desired. Had society's sanctions not so heavily oppressed us and our fears of getting caught not so scared us, perhaps we would have expressed our love for each other by making love, and it would have seemed like the most natural thing in the world, exactly what Mother Nature meant for it to be.

Rick and I struggled with our relationship for the next three years, going steady, breaking up, dating others, getting back together again. My junior year of college, his senior, we got engaged and then I willingly—*very* willingly!—surrendered my virginity to him.

I still remember the night Penny, one of my college roommates, came in from a date and sat on the edge of my bed in our darkened dorm room, smoking a cigarette while she told me in giggly wonderment of "doing it" that night for the first time. It was exquisitely painful and everything the songs hinted it should be, she said. She was deliriously happy. After that she and her boyfriend slept together regularly, but discreetly. They married that following summer, in 1966, and promptly had three children. Then they got divorced and I lost track of them.

Rick and I married in 1967 and divorced in 1979, another statistic in the highest wave of divorce ever to sweep this country. In retrospect I think our marriage was right, and I think our divorce was right. We have managed to be friends these past years, with our daughter's welfare our first priority.

While we have both happily remarried, we will always be an important part of each other's past. I was a girl when I met him and grew up during the course of our relationship. We shared difficulties and triumphs and heartache and joy—the ingredients of any courtship and marriage.

One of the best of times was that wonderful summer of 1963. Revolution was in the air and in just a few months JFK would be assassinated and Vietnam would explode, but that summer the locusts sang in the trees and the night breeze was gentle and the world was full of possibilities when the touch of his hand, his smile, and his kisses were the most glorious things in the world.

And lest I forget, I was sixteen—just the age of my two daughters.

Jay's Turn

I was twelve when my father gave me his one and only piece of advice about women: "Don't ever trust them; they'll screw you every time." He said it with conviction, like Moses handing down the tablets to the Israelites, as he was dropping me off at home after one of our weekend visits together.

My parents divorced in 1955 when divorce was still frowned upon. I was then seven and in second grade. I had no idea why my world was suddenly turned upside down. My father was a sharp guy—a bomber pilot in World War II, then an architect. He flew his own small plane, fixed cars, built buildings, taught me how to catch a curve ball and how to ride a bike. I was never told why we couldn't live together anymore. I just knew that without a father I felt like a leper. I ranted and raved at my mother for years to let me live with him, hating her for standing between him and me. Deep down I also hated myself, because I always suspected that somehow the divorce was my fault.. No one ever told me that I was just a kid and it didn't have anything to do with me.

We lived on Long Island and I must have been terrible at home, because in fourth grade my mother finally relented and let me live with my father for part of the school year. But it didn't work out. Even though I was thrilled to be with him and we did some exciting things together, I never felt that we were building anything permanent. I got the feeling he didn't really want me, that he viewed my stay as temporary.

And it was. I don't remember why, but after a few months with my father I went to live with my grandmother in Florida for a while and then returned home to my mother and younger brother and sister. I was in three different schools that fourth-grade year.

When I was in the eighth grade, my mother remarried, ending my disgrace as a kid whose parents were divorced. By then the drive to live with my father had just about died out. He had remarried and was building a life with a new wife and children, and he wasn't adding any extra rooms onto his house for me or my brother and sister. We had occasional visits with him on weekends, and it was on the way home from one such visit that he dropped the "don't trust women" line. Probably he and my mother had just had a fight about money or something and he was popping off.

Before, I took all his pronouncements as absolute truths. But I had spent the first decade of my life angry at my mother for keeping me from my father, consumed with guilt that he had left home because of me, and working very hard to show him I was a good kid worthy of his love. I had entrusted him with my fantasies and boyhood dreams, only to find that he really didn't want me. Now here he was, whining about what women will do to you.

Something very significant happened to me during that ride home. It probably explains why today I trust women far more than men. I dismissed my father and the years I'd spent trying to please him—attempts that invariably ended in disappointment. It was time to stop trying to define myself through him. I switched my focus to girls and my friends and entered one of the greatest periods of my life.

I'd always had girlfriends, and it seemed like I was always kissing or getting kissed. I had a girlfriend in kindergarten who liked to drag me into a closet to kiss. I think she was older than I was and she definitely knew more than I did.

My first real girlfriend was Jessie. In fifth grade she could run faster, jump higher, and throw or hit a ball farther than anybody in the school. I was very athletic and she was every bit my equal. I liked that. We were best friends during the school year.

That summer one of our classmates held a formal "boy-girl" party. For most of the evening we all ran around. But during the last hour of the party, people began to play slow-dancing music— Ricky Nelson, Elvis Presley, the Platters. I had spent much of the afternoon over at a friend's house getting dancing lessons from his mother. Everything was perfect: the summer night air, the lush trees and party lights, the slow music. It was the first time I ever danced with girls and I enjoyed it. Jessie was there and we danced several times. Something very special happened as we danced. It was a feeling different from the rough-and-tumble play that we normally did. I remember that parents were calling their kids and we knew we would have to leave. We didn't want the moment to end. Jessie said goodbye and left to go with her parents. After a few minutes she came running back and asked me if I would kiss her. I said yes and did.

From that moment our relationship took on a new meaning. We were together through sixth and into seventh grade. We didn't kiss or make out. We behaved more like twins. We could read each other's minds and enjoyed each other's company. It was the type of magic that happens when a relationship develops during the transition between childhood and early adolescence—innocent love, free of the complexities that maturing sexuality would introduce.

During the beginning of sixth grade, a group of us boys from the neighborhood began to take an interest in our own budding sexuality. It was like we all discovered our penises at the same time. There was no shame or fear. We felt more like young scientists: "Hey, look what this thing can do! Let's see how long it takes to do it. Who can do it first?" Over a brief period of time we explored masturbation and then dropped it and moved on. It all seemed quite normal.

About that time I remember that one of my friends found several reels of pornographic films. We watched them with utter fascination. It was stimulating; we got to see the anatomy and how to use it. Unfortunately, we saw sex used aggressively and we saw women reduced to the status of objects, a message that can't help but produce confusion and conflict for males.

When my mother remarried during my eighth grade year, we moved to a small town on the north shore of Long Island. In the early part of the century the area had been called the "Gold Coast" because of all the wealthy families—like the Woolworths, the Morgans, and the Roosevelts—who lived there. The area consisted of estates, woods, fields, water, and beaches. The towns were all small and picturesque. We moved into a beautiful house situated on four acres of lawn and trees that ran down to a small harbor off Long Island Sound. Life seemed idyllic. It was still a safe world. You could walk the streets and cut through estates or through the woods and never worry about your safety. It was a playground for children and teens.

After moving and entering eighth grade, I spent most of the year just making friends. I liked girls and found it easy to communicate with them as friends. But by the latter half of the school year it seemed that boyfriend-girlfriend intrigues were consuming everybody's time. Rumors were always running through the school about this person liking that person. It was very exciting. "Let's see if I can get this person to like me." Notes were sent, phone calls made. Soon two people became an item. Most of the relationships dissolved after a couple of walks or a movie. We were just warming up.

Discovering that you could connect with the opposite sex was like an exciting game. The first step was to become interested in someone. Then you had to let her know. Notes and friends were very helpful. If you were lucky, the other person would express interest in you. This part was the most exciting. An entire week could be consumed with the suspense of the chase. Once the chase was over, things got somewhat awkward. Now you had to do something with this person while everyone else watched and waited. Lusting after someone is relatively easy; trying to talk to that person when you have absolutely nothing in common can be quite a task. If things clicked and the conversation part was manageable, you would progress on to the "magic moment" and the kiss.

Actually, by the end of eighth grade, we were pretty good at getting to the magic moment and quite accomplished in heavy necking and petting. Rarely did anyone go much further. There were enough fears out there to stop us. We repeated the chase routine on through ninth grade.

I was doing several things during this period. First, I was practicing the "how to meet a girl" routine and I was learning about
the types of girls I liked and didn't like. Each time I went with
another girl I became more comfortable with the whole process of
establishing a relationship. And I liked it. I enjoyed the communication and intimacy of the relationship.

Since I no longer considered my parents to be among the living, I invested most of my energy and needs in my relationships.
My mother and stepfather didn't understand what was going on in
my life. I didn't understand theirs any better. Sometimes they
seemed to like each other, and at other times the household was
full of tension. But neither parent paid much attention to me, so I
began to find companionship in the girls I went out with.

In ninth grade I entered a brand-new high school where my
class of 150 students would be the first to graduate. It was 1962—a
time when teachers still commanded some respect and getting an
education was a serious goal. I was a solid "B" student. Sports were
big on Long Island and I lettered in track, football, and
gymnastics.

When my mother and stepfather had married, I had gained a
stepsister who was my age. She now helped me meet other kids
and we got along quite well. At one point we got interested in each
other's best friend. Once when our parents told us they were going
out of town for the day, my stepsister and I decided to make good
use of our empty house. We said goodbye to our parents on a Saturday morning and then walked to the end of the road to meet our
friends. When we got back to the house, we sat in my room and
talked for a while and then my stepsister and her boyfriend went
next door into my brother's room. My girlfriend and I stretched out
on the bed and began to neck.

Suddenly the door to my room opened and my mother and
stepfather stood there. Outside of our shoes, I don't think my girl-

friend or I had removed or undone anything, but I knew we were
cooked. All I could think to do was deflect their attention, so I
pointed to my brother's door and said, "They're in there." When
my stepfather opened the door, I heard someone fall off the bed.
My stepfather marched my stepsister and my friend into my room.
I noticed his glasses were completely fogged up and I struggled to
keep from laughing. My stepfather had a violent temper and my
mother could also get pretty irrational. I knew the potential for disaster was close at hand, but when I saw those glasses and the confused looks on my parents' faces, something told me we would
survive. We got some hasty, on-the-spot lectures and then we were
told to walk our friends to the end of the road and come back and
spend the rest of the day at home. We all looked properly shamed
while we walked to the end of the driveway. Once we got beyond
the fence, I turned to my friend and asked him how his glasses got
so fogged up. With that, we all burst into laughter. The rest of the
walk we relived the entire episode in comedic detail. My stepsister
and I knew we would be in for some parent-teen lectures, but in a
way it had been worth it.

My parents never did give a good explanation of why they came
back again so soon. Even if they hadn't returned, I don't think
much more than some heavy kissing and petting would have occurred. These were still exploratory relationships. Also, the social
prohibition against sexual intercourse when you were in eighth or
ninth grade was very strong. Access to birth control was non-
existent. We knew how far we could go, but we hadn't learned it
from our parents.

My mother did talk to me after that incident. She was concerned and nonthreatening. She didn't give me any valuable information about sex or relationships, she just asked me to be careful
and not do anything that would ruin my life—without telling me

how to avoid doing so. I was still on my own, traveling into the land of teen sexuality without a road map.

And that's how it was for me throughout high school. The adults in my life were either too embarrassed or too ignorant to talk to me. Consequently, I never went to them. I don't know where they thought I would get the information.

Throughout ninth grade the necking and petting became more serious. Hands slipped under sweaters or blouses more readily. Most of the time things got so hot we had to stop before we passed out—one of nature's safety valves. It wouldn't last much longer. By the end of ninth grade there were very few boundaries left short of actually doing it.

Still, fear kept us in line. I don't remember ever having philosophical discussions with anyone about whether people our age were mature enough to handle a sexual relationship. Many of us had gone to the very edge, loved it, and wanted more.

Fortunately, most girls were still willing to throw on the brakes. I think we boys counted on that. It was our form of birth control. I don't remember hearing girls talk about sex, but boys were generating a good deal of peer pressure to do it. When we were together, it was "How far did you get? Did you get under her blouse? Did you get your fingers wet?" Things were building. It was a race. A degree of competition had entered into our lives: Who would be the first to get laid? It was unfortunate because it meant you had to view girls as objects—the means to winning a game.

I felt a great deal of conflict over this issue. I didn't like what the competition did to my relationships with girls but I didn't want to lose the game. At the beginning of tenth grade one of my best friends came sauntering up to our group of male friends and told us about a "nymphomaniac" he had had sex with over the weekend. We all listened intently, secretly envious that he had found every guy's dream—a girl who loved to have sex without any strings attached. When he asked if any of us had gotten laid yet, we all nodded like veterans. Of course he didn't believe us, but now the race was really on. I had to do it before he asked me again. I had to be able to answer with the voice of authority.

I started going out with an eleventh-grader. Aside from her being older, her parents worked and didn't get home until five P.M. We spent many an afternoon necking at her house. It didn't take long before we moved into the bedroom, engaged in several sessions of serious necking, and finally surrendered our virginity to each other. I don't remember much about it except that it was over quickly. It was a significant act, however, accompanied by a great deal of tenderness. I liked her. She was sweet and she cared about me. Unfortunately, she was very shy and rather boring and the relationship didn't last long. Our breakup was not traumatic, just inevitable. We didn't have any contact with each other afterward. But even though the relationship didn't last, the memory did and it's always been very special.

I think that with the first sexual encounter, the buildup is far more significant than the act. It was for me. It takes human beings a long time and a lot of practice to make the most of lovemaking. You need patience, fantasy, and communication between two people for it to be its best. It needs to be *intimate*, and you can't have that with a casual acquaintance. Those early sexual encounters for teens are nice—unless they're not mutually consensual—but they're more like a tickle than an explosion. That's what comes with experience.

I never told the other guys after I did it that first time. Once you do it, you don't need to brag about it—at least that was how I felt. I knew and that was enough. I decided I wasn't going to compromise a girl's reputation by saying anything, and I never did.

I was now fully into the dating scene, and I always dated one

girl at a time. It was just my nature. I approached each relationship as though it was something special and often dated a girl for
an extended period. Even if the relationship cooled down for a
while, it sometimes heated up again later. My goal was to find
someone I was attracted to and could establish a close relationship
with rather than counting numbers. Sometimes sex was part of
these relationships and sometimes not. Some girls made it clear
that they would not engage in sex, and I accepted that. I was not
in relationships that were driven by sex. I was interested in the
intimacy.

Too many parents have a tendency to believe teens are after sex
and nothing else, but that was not my experience. For lots of
them, it's the relationship that matters, and sex, although an important part of the relationship, is not critical.

My high school class had a little bit of everything: jocks, egg-
heads, fruitcakes, goons who worked on cars, beauty queens—you
name it. I knew kids who would marry their high school sweet-
hearts and get a job and start a family minutes after getting their
diploma—if they got one. I was in sports and headed toward college and a career. My personal goals affected my outlook on relationships, the type of girl I found attractive, and how long our
relationship lasted.

I was in the middle of tenth grade when I overheard some of
my friends talking about a ninth-grader who was a knockout. I
went over to the ninth-grade side of the school to find her. When I
did, I was stopped cold. Kelly was blond and beautiful and carried
herself like she knew exactly where she was going. I had never seen
a girl like this on the senior-high side. Introductions were made
and I started to spend time on the ninth-grade side talking with
her.

Kelly was light-years ahead of the ninth-grade boys and a natural for going out with an upperclassman. She came from a well-to-

do family in Brookville. Apart from her looks, what attracted me to her was that she had spunk, intelligence, class, and a razor-sharp tongue. She was not dependent on our relationship, which meant that we operated as equals—a new experience for me.

I liked her family and they liked me. I spent a lot of time at their house and often felt like a son. I would use the tractor to cut the lawn and even painted their house as a summer job. They had a boat and loved skiing and we would spend entire days skiing on Long Island Sound.

Kelly was precocious in many areas and necking certainly was one of them. The thing that made her so different from all the other girls I went out with was the way she drew the line. It was obvious that she enjoyed making out—in fact, she had been la-beled a tease before I started to go out with her. It took me a little while to understand that even though she enjoyed the intensity as much as I did, she had no intention of letting things go beyond a certain point.

We went steady for a while. During that time we talked about sex. She wanted to know all about it, but she wasn't about to do it. Part of it was fear. Mainly it was because she had a goal of being a virgin when she got married. She enjoyed making out and knew she would enjoy sex, but it would be on her terms and in her time.

I was impressed with her determination and self-control. It also made our relationship safe. I have to admit that most of the time I acted like a car without brakes. But even brakeless cars run out of gas, and eventually our relationship sputtered and stalled. We tried to pick it up again during my senior year, but it wasn't the same. I think too much time had passed. Her rules about the belt line had weakened just a bit, but she was still a virgin when I left for college.

Abstinence was the only way to make sure a girl wouldn't get pregnant. None of them were using the pill yet, and we guys couldn't get condoms. I tried once. A friend and I went to a neighboring town where we didn't know anybody and waited outside a drugstore until we knew no customers were inside. Then I stumbled over to the prescription counter where the pharmacist was stocking shelves and mumbled to him that I wanted a box of Trojans. He ignored me. I tried again, this time speaking louder, but even though I knew he heard me, he continued to act as though he hadn't. A customer came in and I had to retreat, my mission unsuccessful.

None of my friends or I had been told anything about sex by our parents—everybody was too embarrassed to talk about it—and the schools certainly didn't tell us anything. No one helped us understand all those feelings and that strong sex drive and what we were supposed to do about it, so we did what came naturally.

I suppose some girls in my school got pregnant, though none in my circle of friends did. Because it was an affluent area, it's certainly possible that there were some abortions or girls going off to visit an aunt and uncle for a few months. I just don't remember. As far as we guys were concerned, it was up to the girl to know if it was a "safe" time of the month. There was no discussion about it.

The relationship between my mother and stepfather began to go sour shortly after they married. My stepfather was used to getting his way. So was my mother. Then there were us kids. No one knew much back then about making blended families work. Sides were drawn early in the marriage, and the house was actually divided into two camps, with our family at one end and my stepfather and stepsister at the other. My stepfather drank daily, and when agitated, he drank too much. Words got exchanged and fights broke out. My mother, my brother, my sister, and I spent three Christmases in a row at a motel. My mother and stepfather would get into a fight, the police would come, and we would have to leave the house for our own safety. After several weeks my mother and stepfather would reconcile and we would move back home. But it was never very good. The barriers between our families were becoming permanent, and we tried to stay out of each other's way. Living together was no longer fun. In fact, the booze and level of hostility made it very explosive.

As a teen I felt my only recourse was to take care of myself and keep my distance from my stepfather. My mother was sleeping longer periods in my sister's room at our end of the house. I began to feel protective of her and to appreciate how hard she had tried over the years to create a home for my brother, sister, and me while married to two difficult men.

This was a dark period in my life. The tension at home was getting to me. I found some relief by building an underground retreat. It was a room measuring six by eight feet and had recessed sleeping berths on each wall. The ceiling height was about six feet. The entire structure was made from plywood and assorted lumber and hidden from the main house by a stand of pine trees. It took several weeks to hand-dig the hole so that the roof line was just at ground level. I could come and go from the retreat without being seen from the house. During the winter I heated it with a small cast-iron Franklin stove that I bought in Locust Valley and carried home. It was perfect.

I started to go out with Connie during the eleventh grade. We both were involved in track. She was a very good runner and that impressed me. As tense as my home life was, hers was worse. Her parents always seemed to be at odds. Her older sister had dropped out of school to have a baby, and her younger siblings were starting to run out of control.

Shortly after we started going out, Connie's mother walked out of the cramped little house they lived in and moved to Florida.

She left everything, including all the kids. Connie's dad seemed hopelessly defeated.

Connie was an athlete and very strong and often we would get into all-out wrestling matches on the living room floor that were actually sexual foreplay. She had a quirky, unpredictable personality that gave our relationship a touch of excitement. It was easy for me to get out of the house at night. Sometimes I just said I was going to sleep out in my retreat in the backyard. Connie's father didn't pay any attention at all to her. The conditions were perfect for developing a sexual relationship. We were both dealing with unstable home environments and felt that we had been let down by the adults in our lives. As teen lovers so often do, we gave each other the physical and emotional support that we knew our parents weren't getting in their relationships. Both Connie and I had plenty of free time, we had places to go to be alone, and sex easily became an active part of our relationship.

Connie and I stayed together through eleventh grade. By the start of my senior year we had stopped seeing each other on a steady basis. Occasionally, after having too many beers, I would go over to Connie's house and wake her up by throwing rocks at her window. Enough beers used to make me very sentimental—and horny. Most of the time she would let me in and I would sneak into her room where we would talk, snuggle, and have sex if I didn't pass out first. By five A.M. she would wake me up and send me on my way. I would sneak back into my own house or go to sleep down in my retreat. It's amazing what boys can get away with. From what I see today, it hasn't changed at all.

My life during my last year at high school was dedicated to being a senior. I received final letters in football, gymnastics, and track. Our track season ended with a league championship, and I went to the state meet in the shot put. I lived sports that last year. I was also sending out college applications and preparing to leave Locust Valley. My future was out there somewhere, and I didn't have much interest in starting a serious relationship.

So my senior year was free of the intense relationships that marked preceding years. Mostly I would go out once or twice with one of my prior girlfriends—just for fun.

My high school years concluded with an event that stays with me to this day. Our town and school were small enough that we kids all knew one another. We grew up together and attended the same school. Vincent was different from the rest of us. He was effeminate and had been called queer for as long as I could remember. Both Vincent and his "best friend" lived on the working-class side of town. They acted like an old married couple and would often get into incredible squabbles in school. It was amazing to watch them. Their behavior just added fuel to the teasing they received. Most of the time Vincent stood his ground. When someone would ask him if he gave blow jobs, he would roll his eyes, toss his head back, and walk away with a great flourish. It was such an amusing response that guys would ask him just to see him get angry. The guys could get merciless in the shower room. Several times I couldn't stand it and had to tell people to knock it off. No one ever tried to hurt Vincent physically. In part that was due to our small-town mentality. Had someone from another town tried to hurt him, we would have stood up for him.

After years of kidding, taunting, teasing, and sharing the same classes, Vincent and I had a somewhat comfortable, although often testy, acquaintance. I was secure enough in my identity to be friends with him.

Several weeks before graduation, Vincent came up to me in the hallway when I was getting a drink at the fountain.

"Hi, Jay," he said. That in itself was rather unusual, because Vincent usually didn't have anything to say to anybody. It was

clear that he had something on his mind. He seemed quite agitated. He shuffled back and forth from one foot to another, and finally he blurted out, "You want to go out with me?"

At first it didn't dawn on me what he meant. When it did, I
found myself feeling touched. I knew he was serious. Over the
years I had come to like Vincent. I liked his grit and I knew he
was a good person. I wouldn't have traded places with him for a
million dollars, but I did admire his style. Given my past history
with girls, I didn't have any question about my sexual orientation,
so I thanked him and declined the offer. He accepted that and
went on his way.

What happened afterward burned the incident permanently into
my memory. I must have told one of my friends about Vincent's
invitation—a kind of "oh, by the way" comment. About a week
later Vincent came up to me with real pain and hurt in his face
and tears in his eyes and demanded to know how I could dare tell
anyone about what he said to me.

At that moment I realized that he had been very sincere about
wanting to go out with me and that I had hurt him deeply by sharing my refusal with someone else and inadvertently humiliating
him. I felt that I had betrayed a human being and it didn't feel
good. I learned from Vincent. He taught me tolerance for people
whose sexuality is different from the mainstream. I don't know how
his life went after we left high school. I hope he didn't have to go
through the agony and abuse most homosexuals suffer.

I graduated with gusto in June 1966. In spite of my family
problems, I enjoyed my teen years. I think part of the reason they
went as well as they did is because I had strong goals and a lot of
encouragement from my mother and grandmother. I really believed I had a future.

College was a different story. I didn't date much after high
school. I went to an all-male college, and for a long period of time

I was in situations where it was impossible to meet women. High school had made it easy. The real world didn't. Also, I had a hard time finding my niche in life. For a while I dropped out of college, got into the drug scene, and fell prey to depression and anger. Once I lost sight of my goals, I drifted for years, eventually getting back on track, but not before a short-lived marriage and fatherhood.

By going back into my past, I have put myself in touch once again with how it feels to be a teenager—how unsettling a time it is, how many dangers and obstacles there are, and how important parental support is.

Reflecting on what I did and how I felt makes me want to communicate in a whole new way with my children. I want to know about their beliefs, thoughts, and experiences. I want to be able to use my experiences to help guide and advise them instead of being an obstacle they've got to get around in their journey to adulthood.

I want to share with them what I experienced and how I felt during those few sweet years of my teens when the whole world of dating and love and sex was high drama. I want to express to them the angst, the exhilaration, and that it was the best and worst of times. I want to be honest with them and tell them that sex was only a part of it, but a natural part that worked well because I never hurt anyone and because for me sex was always part of a loving relationship.

And I want to tell them I have no regrets. If I can be their guide, their friend, their advocate, and their parent, I will help them to enter adulthood able to look back and say the same thing.

When the two of us sat down to read each other's remembrance, both of us were anxious to share our own and curious to read each other's.

By the time we had finished we were both smiling. Sometimes we had been close to tears, other times we had laughed. We had nodded our heads when struck by some insight into the other. We were eager in some instances to question further and to ask for more detail.

We could see the similarities. Though raised in very different families in different parts of the country, both of us had felt alienated from our families. We both had strong goals that kept us progressing forward. We were eager to experiment with relationships and self-assured enough to do so.

Both of us felt that we had little actual information about sex while we were teenagers. In Newman Grove, the mentality of the early sixties was similar to that of the fifties elsewhere, and most girls remained virginal if they didn't want a shotgun wedding. On Long Island in the early sixties, guys were assuming that girls were watching the calendar and taking care of birth control. Otherwise, there were lots of similarities in our middle-class teenage years. Both of us wish we'd had more contact with our parents. Both of us are grateful that we didn't suffer any sexual traumas (pregnancy, abuse, disease) while we were teens.

By the time we finished our reading, we had a new understanding of each other and a new closeness that has affected many areas of our lives, not the least of which is how we will approach issues with our daughters in the future. And both of us now feel much more in touch with our daughters and what they are going through. Yes, the times change, and that *does* make a difference. But people and feelings don't.

We recommend this exercise in going back to all parents. But give it some time. It's like peeling back the layers of an onion. One memory will trigger others and slowly you will remember your teen years.

Good luck—and enjoy!

CHAPTER 6

WHEN SONS OR DAUGHTERS ARE GAY OR LESBIAN

Because of our limited exposure to homosexuality, and with so much consciousness-raising going on in our society about what it means to be a lesbian woman or gay man, we knew we couldn't honestly explore the issue of teens and sex without some insight into the 10 to 15 percent who fall outside the heterosexual mainstream.

When we had visited with Steve Walker's group of students, he had invited us to attend a support group for gay and lesbian teens.

"The students you've talked to are fairly average," he said. "You had a good gender and racial mix and they come from all kinds of homes in terms of income, single parents, blended families, and so forth. They're a good cross section—except that they don't represent the segment of the population that is homosexual. If you want to know about the full spectrum of teens and sex, you must know this group, too. Sex is just as big an issue for them, and because of the conflict most of them feel, it's even more difficult. It's usually during the teen years that they confront and try to work through their sexual identity."

We jumped at his offer to visit the support group and set a time.

Passages meets on Sunday evenings in Kansas City at the Good Samaritan headquarters, a hospice for people with AIDS. Anywhere from ten to thirty young people, mostly males, attend the meetings. The programs are sometimes informational, sometimes strictly fun, and always supportive.

When we arrived, our first perception was that these kids looked just like the high school groups we'd talked to. The notable exception was that two of the boys were holding hands. Otherwise, some of them were shy and quiet, others were bold and funny, some were good-looking, some were not. Some were stylishly dressed, others looked punk. Some jumped right into the conversation, some held back. We immediately liked them. As they told us their stories, we listened attentively.

"Do us a favor and don't use the term 'sexual preference,' " a boy said to us as we started to visit with them. "Please use 'sexual orientation.' Homosexuality is not something you choose."

We thanked him for the suggestion and followed it. We also commented that experts still seemed divided on the nature-versus-nurture issue. Some of the latest findings suggested genetic prebirth influences, while others support the nature-nurture combination theory. At this point, there is no definitive answer.

"Just so you don't think it's the old stereotype of passive fathers and dominating mothers or a result of being sexually molested," the boy said, "Everybody knows that isn't true."

"Or that we chose it. Why would anybody *choose* this?" another boy remarked. "My gay and lesbian friends all say that if they had a choice they would be straight. Lots of people hate you if you're gay. You can't live openly many places. We're frequently targets of violence. But we're going to be whatever we are, so it's just a question of how we're going to live."

"All this research to find out if it's genetics or the way you're raised bothers me," a girl said. "Why waste the time? Even in the homosexual community they're looking for reasons why they are the way they are instead of just accepting it. Nobody's out there trying to figure out why people are heterosexual. Why are people trying to find something to blame this on?"

"The only reason I would change is because of the pressure," said the boy next to her. "I really wish I could be treated like everyone else. I wish I could fit in. I always got beat up at school."

"We all did," said another boy. "Ever since I was in kindergarten, I've been called a fag. Kids would follow me around, shouting it at me. I didn't even know what it meant when it started. It stopped in high school because I dated a guy on the football team. He was big and mean." He paused and looked away. "He committed suicide last year after he came out to his parents. They completely rejected him and he couldn't handle it."

"It takes a long time to get comfortable with yourself," a young man said. "I'm twenty now. I've known about myself since I was fourteen and had my first lover. I always knew I didn't like girls, but until this guy came on to me, I didn't know what I was. I was eighteen when I finally told my parents. I had to move out because they were so upset that they couldn't stand to have me in the house. A lot of times parents don't suspect because we learn early to keep up very good appearances."

"If you say you'd change, it's only because you're trying to please your parents," a soft-spoken boy said. "I'm sixteen. I think I knew when I was five that I was different. I really wanted to be the same. I even dated girls and I denied all those feelings I had for other guys. I thought a lot about never coming out and just not having any kind of relationships. But then I thought about how unhappy I would be being alone and how much I wanted to love someone.

"When I finally told my parents last year, they tried to bargain with me. They sent me to a shrink, but finally I said, 'This is the way I am. I would change if I could, but I can't.' " His eyes filled with pain. "So they said, 'Then you're not part of this family anymore. Pack your bags and get out.' So now I'm on my own. I live with friends."

"That's why I can't come out to my parents," another boy said. "The same thing would happen. They couldn't take it."

"When I told my mom," a girl commented, "she had a nervous breakdown. She made me promise not to ever tell my dad. I think she's scared he'll kick me out. When she got out of the hospital, she told me she couldn't talk to me about it and not to bring it up. She tries to ignore it but I know she thinks about it and I know she isn't comfortable when I'm playing with my little sister."

"I really want to tell my mother, but then she would tell my father and I don't want him to know," a boy said. "I'm eighteen and I plan to go to college next year. My dad said he'd pay for college and buy me a car and I don't want to risk that, so I'm going to have to wait till I'm out on my own."

"Even if you come out five years from now, they're going to pressure you to not be gay," a boy told him. "My mom knows and she keeps saying, 'I don't think you're all-the-way gay. You still have tendencies toward girls and you don't know it.' I said to her, 'Mom! How many years do I have to go through this before you can accept it?' Why do parents have to act like assholes about it when they find out? We're the ones who have to live with this, not them."

"If your parents can't accept you for what you are, get away from them," another boy said. "A parent's love is supposed to go beyond who you have sex with. A parent is supposed to love you no matter what. My parents' marriage broke up over me because my mom tried to support me and my dad had a fit and said I was going to hell."

"I haven't told my parents yet, because I figure if they want to know, they can ask," said a sullen seventeen-year-old. "It's my sexuality and it has nothing to do with them. As soon as I can be independent, I'll move out and then tell them. I don't care what they think of me. I know how angry they're going to be. My mother will blame herself and it'll be a bad scene. I don't plan to be there for it."

"My mom blames herself. There's a lot of guilt if you don't understand it," a boy said. "She said she knew since I was a little kid, but she tried to change me by making me go out for all the sports and putting me in Boy Scouts. I told her it wasn't her fault, but she doesn't believe it."

"My mother ended up going to a psychologist to help her get over it," a girl of nineteen said. "She's done okay with it. She even went to a Gay Pride parade. I came out to her last year and she said, 'Yeah, I knew that.' I said, 'Then why didn't you tell me? I've gone through hell!' "

"My parents are divorced and I live with my father," a sixteen-year-old boy said. "When I came out to him two years ago, he said, 'What can I do to fix it?' And I said, 'It's not like I have a broken leg. It's not something that will heal.' Actually, it's brought us closer together. He's trying to understand. He lets my boyfriend stay over-night and he fixes us breakfast in the morning."

"My parents won't let my boyfriend stay overnight, even though they know we're lovers and they say they're comfortable with it," another sixteen-year-old said. "It really annoys me. I get the feeling they think we aren't anything but little sex machines. They don't realize that our relationship is more than sex."

"My mother won't let my boyfriend spend the night, either," a twenty-one-year-old said, "but she also won't let my sister's boyfriend stay. I told my mother last year that I was gay. I asked her if she wanted me to move out and she said no. I asked if she had any questions, and then we talked for half a day. She asked me everything about it. She asked me if it hurts," he said with a wink, causing everyone in the circle to burst into laughter.

"My mom says anal sex is disgusting, and I told her, 'Don't knock it till you've tried it,' " a boy said, giggling. "And she said she had.

I about had a heart attack. My mom loves my friends. When I told her I was gay a couple of years ago when I was fifteen, I thought it was going to be real tough. But she just said, 'It's okay. I thought maybe you were.'"

"My mother said, 'I don't like it, but I gave birth to you and you're mine.' At first she asked me to not live the lifestyle, but I told her that I was already out of the closet and planned to stay out," the twenty-one-year-old said. "She begs me to be careful. I am. My boyfriend and I don't show affection in public, but I wish we could. Lots of times I want to take his hand or snuggle with him in the movies. That's why it's nice to go to a gay bar, because then you can show your feelings for each other."

"My parents don't live together. They both know I'm gay," a boy said. "It doesn't matter at my mom's house, but at Dad's I don't show any affection for my boyfriend. Dad wouldn't be able to handle it. He'd lose it. He'd threaten to either cut off my nuts or my boyfriend's. I'm sixteen now and I had my first lover when I was thirteen. I'd already tried sex with a girl and didn't like it. But with that first guy— wow! The feelings were so different. It was so much more emotional, so much more than sex. It was full-blown emotion. I didn't want to live a day without him."

"I've never been with a girl," the boy next to him said. "I just couldn't. I've always had homosexual tendencies, way back in grade school. The boys would call me 'sweetmeat.' I came out to myself this past year when I was fifteen, but I haven't told my parents yet. They're religious and they'll want me to pray to be changed. I can't change. This is what I am. I think they may kick me out. I have to be prepared for that. Maybe I'll never tell them—but I hate living a lie."

"I think bisexuals have the hardest path, because they don't know what they are and they have to choose one or the other and might not be happy with it," a girl said. "I'm a lesbian, and I'm not going to be able to tell my parents either. I love them, so I've got to protect them because I think it would kill my dad. I've always been his little sweetheart. I don't know if I'll ever find a partner. I've been with a couple of women, but it didn't work out. You don't have a big field to pick from."

"But you find each other," a boy said encouragingly. "It's weird. I've had a crush on this guy who works in a record store but I never said anything to him because I didn't know for sure about him. Then two weeks ago I saw him at a gay bar and we got to talking and I asked him out."

"I've known since I was seven years old that I'm gay," an eighteen-year-old said. "I went through a period of blaming—that I was molested as a kid, that I was raised in an all-female household with no male role models. It took me until just recently to say, 'Why blame it on anything?' I don't think it can be explained. I've had people come up to me and ask, 'Why are you gay?' and I say, 'Why are you straight?' It's just the way I am."

If you could offer some advice to parents, what would you say? we asked. They all clamored to speak.

"Don't be homophobic and say cruel things about homosexuals," a boy said. "That just makes it harder for everyone."

"If your kid comes out to you, be supportive. And give yourself time to adjust. At least a year," advised another.

"Try to be open," a boy said. "Try to see your child's point of view. Don't say, 'That's wrong,' or 'Why are you doing this to me?' "

"If you suspect your child might be gay, don't force them to tell you," a girl said. "They will when they're ready. Drop hints that it's okay, that you know everyone's not heterosexual and you'll love them no matter what."

"Don't reject them and kick them out," a boy added. "You've got to treat it as normal. They aren't doing this to hurt you. It's just what they are. And accept their friends."

"Let your kid educate you. Ask lots of questions. Most parents don't know anything about being gay," another said. "Tell them it's not their fault. Tell them you were born this way so they'll feel better."

"Let parents know that unhappy gay kids can grow into *happy* gay adults," added one of the oldest participants. "My parents always imagined that my life was very lonely and scary and secretive. It was a great help to them to learn that there was a pleasant community for me to be part of."

Later, after the teenagers left, we spent a few minutes talking to the two sponsors. "Did anything surprise you?" they asked.

"They're terrific people. Bright, highly verbal, funny, open," we said. "They could be anybody's kids. We're impressed by their insight and their maturity."

"On one level that's true," one of the sponsors said, nodding. "They come here and they have a great time. They help one another a lot. In many instances these kids don't have anyone else to talk to outside of this group, so the group really becomes their lifeline. They're only 'out' when they come here.

"But on another level, they're like all teenagers in that they can be irresponsible. They think they're immortal and nothing bad is ever going to happen to them. They all say, 'Yes, we practice safe sex,' but the majority of them don't. We did an anonymous survey and almost all of them told us that condoms were uncomfortable and too much trouble. When it gets down to the heat of the moment, they tell themselves, 'It won't happen to me.' We've done several intensive programs on safe sex, but AIDS is just a matter of time. Once someone in the group tests positive, it will change things."

"And what about their mental health?" we asked. We mentioned that a high school counselor we know expressed to us her concern over gay and lesbian high school students who are confused, isolated, and unhappy. She told us that very few counselors were trained to help this segment of the student body that she termed "too many kids to ignore." The public schools have little, if any, support for them, because school districts can't afford it and officials don't recognize the need for it.

"It's a big problem," the sponsors said. "We're losing too many of these kids to alcohol, drugs, and suicide. Adolescence is a time of soul searching. Homosexual young people kill themselves at three times the rate of heterosexual young people. That's absolutely unacceptable. All we can do for these kids is reach out and let them know we're here and we're available if they ever want to talk."

We had already heard that suicide statistic and we found it very unsettling. Who were we to judge another's sexual orientation? Another's lifestyle? We recalled that during World War II, Hitler had forced homosexuals to wear pink triangles to denote their homosexuality and targeted them for extermination in his death camps, using vicious, hideous methods. But how far have we come? Here in our society, where homosexuals have no civil rights, violence against them is commonplace. As recently as 1992, fine career officers found to be homosexual were dismissed from the military on the grounds that homosexuality is "incompatible with military service." As one example, a colonel with an unblemished record who had been in the National Guard for twenty-seven years and served in Vietnam was discharged because she had admitted to being a lesbian.

Here in Kansas City, as in most places, discrimination in housing and employment is widespread against homosexuals. The Kansas City annual Gay Pride Parade is a cause of both celebration and concern. After the last one, an irate citizen wrote to the editor of the *Kansas City Star* that homosexuality is "a perversion, an unnatural manifestation of sexual desire for one of the same sex."

On the *700 Club* on television, Pat Robertson recently referred to homosexuality as "an abomination of the Lord," saying that those who practice it are taking a "plunge toward sexual suicide."

The Vatican in July 1992 termed homosexuality "an objective disorder," comparing it to mental illness, and voiced its support of discrimination against homosexuals in such areas as health benefits, public housing, and the hiring of teachers, coaches, and military personnel.

We heard high school students voice fears of gays and lesbians, saying such things as "You have to watch out for them. They'll try to hit on you." "They might try to turn you." "I don't respect them."

We saw a long, rambling letter an aunt had written her young adult nephew when she learned he was gay and HIV-positive. It brought home to us how this issue can divide families. Among her statements were these:

> I am very sorry that I can not truthfully feel for you. You have gone against everything that the Almighty God has condemned. I really cannot feel anything for you. My heart aches for the innocent victims of the gays. . . . My prayers are for the innocent not your kind. If I had my way I would find the biggest island and ship all the gays out there and let your kind fend for themselves. They did it to the lepers why not the gays. If God wanted you to be gay he would of made Adam and Steve, not Adam and Eve. . . . The only thing your kind will be remembered for is how many innocent lives you took. I feel God has finally decided to call a halt to all the evil your kind has been doing. . . . And your proud of being gay? I don't know how you can possibly sleep at night knowing what your kind has started. I cannot imagine in my wildest dreams what you have done to your mother and father. Our whole family feels the

same way. I talked to your father and I told him he ought to get a gun and kill you now before more innocent victims die. That would be the most sensible thing to do. If you were my son I know I would find the courage to do it. Your father hung up on me and he was sobbing so hard. You certainly have disgraced both of your parents. . . . And ask yourself why you want to kill them. That's what your doing. I know in my heart your father won't last the year out because you are killing him. He is a beaten man. Your so very lucky that Grandpop Smith is dead. Believe me I know what he would of done and it wouldn't of been so nice.

In 1989 the U.S. Department of Health & Human Services issued the *Report of the Secretary's Task Force on Youth Suicide,* noting that suicide is the leading cause of death in young people who are gay, lesbian, bisexual, and transsexual, and that "gay youth are 2 to 3 times more likely to attempt suicide than other young people. They may comprise up to 30 percent of completed youth suicides annually."

Further, the report stated:

The earlier youth are aware of their orientation and identify themselves as gay, the greater the conflicts they have. Gay youth face problems in accepting themselves due to internalization of a negative self image and the lack of accurate information about homosexuality during adolescence. Gay youth face extreme physical and verbal abuse, rejection and isolation from family and peers. They often feel totally alone and socially withdrawn out of fear of adverse consequences. As a result of these pressures, lesbian and gay youth are more vulnerable than other youth to psychosocial problems including substance abuse, chronic depression, school failure, early relationship conflicts, being forced to leave their families, and having to survive on their own prematurely. Each of these problems represents a risk factor for suicidal feelings and behavior among gay, lesbian, bisexual and transsexual youth.[1]

A study that appeared in *Pediatrics* magazine places the figure for young gay people attempting suicide by age fifteen at 30 percent, with at least half of them trying it more than once.

One young man who attempted suicide unsuccessfully tried to explain how difficult it was growing up in a small Midwest town aware of what he was but knowing no other homosexuals. The only pictures he ever saw were of flamboyant homosexuals, and he knew that wasn't him. All he heard from his family, friends, and church was negative messages. Finally, assuming that there was something seriously wrong with him and that he would never be able to be happy, he saw no recourse but to kill himself.

Shortly after our visit to Passages we heard a local radio call-in show, moderated by a psychologist, featuring two teenagers, one gay and one lesbian, who shared their stories about being homosexual. (Bisexuals, by the way, are a very small percentage of the homosexual population. Usually they will eventually settle on one or the other orientation, though some do try to combine the two lifestyles. Transsexuals are even more rare. A transsexual is physically a male or female who feels he or she is psychologically the other gender, a situation sometimes solved by a sex-change operation. There are also men who like to cross-dress but are not homosexual.)

On the air, the lesbian teenager, who was eighteen, spoke first.

"Before coming out and finding a support group, I felt that I had a deep dark secret I couldn't share with anyone," she said. "I was raised to be religious and I was so scared that God would hate me. I would cry myself to sleep, praying to God to make me straight. I tried very hard. I dated, but I just couldn't feel anything for guys. I knew from the time I was ten that I was attracted to girls. What I am isn't a choice. It's just inside me. I was born this way."

Said the boy, "I think I've known since I was about four, although I didn't understand any of it for a long long time. I never knew a gay person when I was growing up. My hardest time was junior and senior high school. Kids hate anyone who's different, and they knew I was. Those years are when everyone is experimenting with dating and sex. I lived a lie, denying what I was. I even dated some, even though I have no heterosexual feelings at all. But there was no one for me to date who was gay.

"There's nothing in my background that I know of that would have 'made' me gay. It's just me. Now I'm nineteen and since coming out this past year, I've felt so much better about myself because I don't have to pretend anymore. Religion isn't a problem for me. I figure if God didn't want me to be gay, I wouldn't have been born gay. However, I *do* have to worry about gay bashing. I'm always scared of that.

"People seem to think that all homosexuals do is think about sex. But how we have sex and with whom is such a minor part of who and what we are. You can't change what people are. You can't *make* someone into a homosexual, just like you can't *make* someone straight who's gay."

A listener called in to comment that when he was a young teen he was accused of being gay. "After what I went through—and it was awful—my feeling is that nobody would want to wake up one morning and say, 'You know, I think I want a lifestyle where I will go through a lot of abuse for the rest of my life.' I have a lot of empathy for you and I admire you for coming out and being willing to speak publicly. I think the idea that gays recruit others to be gay is ridiculous."

The psychologist moderating the program said, "What our culture needs is straight people talking about these issues as much as gays do. And parents of gay men and lesbians need to speak out. My guess is that they're terrified when they learn they have a gay or lesbian child and that they just wish it could go away." Then she asked her guests, "What advice do you have for parents?"

"Be very open and listen," the girl said. "Your children need someone to understand and to love them. Realize they aren't doing this to hurt you. It's just part of who they are. Parents always think they did something wrong and they want to make it better."

"Don't try to change it," the boy said. "You'll just make things worse. Help them as much as you think you can. And don't stop loving them."

We began to wonder, what *does* happen in a family when the parents learn they have a homosexual child? If 10 to 15 percent of the population is gay or lesbian, then one in ten families in this country has a homosexual son or daughter.

We had heard the unhappy stories—of kids kicked out when they came out to their parents (an estimated one in four); of dysfunctional homosexual adults who were never able to be at peace with themselves, whether or not they chose to remain celibate; of all the AIDS victims who had no families to support and care for them in their illness; of ministers who rail from the pulpit against homosexuals; of the homophobia in our society that leads to violence against homosexuals (20 percent report being the victims of violent assault); and of the societal discrimination that includes being denied the right of same-sex marriage, joint tax returns, and oftentimes recognition as a family unit, even when partners are raising children together.

By now we had heard a number of young people relate their experiences of coming out to their parents—the hardest thing they all said they ever had to do. We knew that many parents disowned their children on the basis of religion and morals.

But we also know that most parents love their kids no matter what, and it was these parents, the ones struggling to accept their homosexual children and the ones who had successfully done this, that we wanted to visit with.

We knew of the support group P-FLAG—Parents and Friends of Lesbians and Gays—and called the information number to locate a chapter near us. There is a P-FLAG chapter in Kansas City, but we were also given the name of a central Kansas chapter organized by Beverly Barbo in Lindsborg, Kansas. That interested us. Lindsborg, located in the central part of the state, has only 3,000 people. Why would someone in so tiny a town organize a chapter?

We called Beverly and found ourselves talking to a remarkable woman who, in the wake of losing her gay son to AIDS, devotes herself as a writer, speaker, and activist to making life better for gay men and lesbians and their families by helping to increase public awareness about homosexuality and AIDS. She has written a very touching book, *The Walking Wounded*, about her son and his death from AIDS. Ironically, it is well known in many parts of the country—and barely known in her hometown.

Beverly and her husband, Dave, invited us to attend their next P-FLAG chapter meeting, and on a hot July Sunday we drove four hours to Salina, Kansas—the chapter's central gathering place—to meet with a dozen parents, several of whom came considerable distances to tell us their stories.

With the exception of Beverly and Dave, we've changed the names here because some of these parents have not told neighbors and friends in the small Kansas towns they live in that they have gay children, and we wanted to respect their privacy.

In attendance along with Beverly and Dave Barbo were people we will call Grace and Robert, who are just retiring from farming; Donna and John, a housewife and a dentist; Eleanor, a librarian whose husband had not come along; Madge, a high school gym teacher, also there without her husband; and Priscilla, whose husband was hospitalized, gravely ill with heart problems.

Like the Barbos, Priscilla lost her homosexual son to AIDS. Madge's beloved nephew is near death with AIDS. Eleanor and the couple Donna and John have adult sons who are gay. Grace and Robert's gay son committed suicide last year. Grace, an unpretentious farm wife, spoke first.

"Our son Jack killed himself after he was fired from a job he loved because they found out he was gay. He'd been fired from other jobs for the same reason, and once he was forced to leave a town. They didn't say on the papers that that was the reason he was fired, of course, but the supervisor told him it was.

"Jack was a nurse. He had a gift with the old people and they really loved him.

"He'd had a hard time about being a little feminine, ever since he was a little boy. He was always small for his age and he was sick a lot. We were real close. It's so hard for me that I wasn't there the night he . . .

"I hadn't suspected about him being gay. He always seemed fine as far as I was concerned—so he finally had to tell me. That was three years ago when he was twenty-one. For a long time I couldn't tell anybody. I was so ashamed. I kept wondering what I'd done wrong. But Jack kept saying, 'It wasn't anything you did, Mom.' He wrote that in his suicide note, too.

"When I was finally getting better about him being gay, he took his dad and me to a gay bar in Topeka because he wanted us to meet some of his friends. When he introduced us, he said to them, 'My mom and dad know and they still love me.' You ought to have seen those young men. They were so handsome. The good Lord gives these people something extra. There's no kidding about it. They're talented, good-looking, loving, and more considerate than other people. They've got something others don't have. Jack was real special."

Grace's husband, Robert, a large, lumbering man in overalls who looks like the farmer he is, listened carefully, then added, "When I learned about Jack being gay, I was really shocked. I sure wasn't pleased. I'd made plenty of snide remarks about gay people in my time and I figured he could change if he wanted to. But he moved away and I got to reading whatever I saw in the newspaper or magazines and I saw a couple of those talk shows on the TV. I got to understanding more and I realized that that's the way they're born. Of course my attitude changed."

Robert fought back tears as he continued. "I think before you discuss anything, you've got to educate yourself and get comfortable with an issue. So the next time we saw each other and got to talking about it, why, I talked a lot different. Before, I was right and he was wrong and that was all there was to it. So it made a difference in our relationship."

"When you talk about how good your son was, you could be talking about mine," Priscilla said quietly. "Alan was one of five children, and when he was a teenager, I found some poetry he had written revealing that he was gay. I didn't tell anyone, not even my husband. I guess I hoped it would go away. His brothers and sisters would joke behind his back about him being gay but I wouldn't say anything. I would watch and somehow I just knew he was.

"When Alan was a senior in high school, I confronted him. He told me he had known since he was a tiny child that he was different. But I said that he needed to change himself. I told him to get therapy and get his act together because he was going off to college the next year. I realize now how ignorant and hurtful and unhelpful I was and I'm very sorry about that.

"He wanted to change and he almost got married. I knew that would be a disaster, and I told him I would tell the girl if he didn't. So he did, but she said she wanted to marry him anyway. She thought she could change him. Fortunately for both of them, he called it off.

"We'd known for several years that Alan was HIV-positive. He'd been living in Phoenix, working as a musician. He had a roommate and was happy there. When he told us he was HIV-positive, he expected us to reject him. Quite the opposite—everyone was very supportive. But we didn't know he had developed full-blown AIDS until his roommate called last winter and said Alan was dying and wanted to come home.

"My husband was very ill with his heart problems, so one of my daughters and I went out to get him. It was awful. He was so sick. . . . But we got him home and our doctor agreed to treat him. Quite remarkable for such a small town. We tried to care for him at home but couldn't. We had to put him in a nursing home and he went downhill rapidly. He died a month ago. He was thirty-one."

As Donna put a comforting arm around Priscilla, she began to tell her own story. "Our son Kip is twenty-four. He's a graphic artist and lives in New York. We've known since he was seventeen that he's gay. I heard a friend of his make a reference to Kip being gay just before Christmas in Kip's senior year of high school. I was floored. I confronted him and he said he was pretty convinced he was. I said, 'It's not a problem with me, and I know it's okay with God, but I don't know what we're going to do about your dad.'

"I went to our minister for counseling and he told me homosexuality wasn't natural. I tried to check out some books at the public library, but they were all out—which I thought was interesting. Finally I couldn't stand it any longer and I told John. I just blurted it out. He said, 'That doesn't surprise me.'" She laughed. "I'd gone through weeks of agony, and he was very accepting of it. I didn't expect our daughter, who was fourteen at the time, to have any trouble with it. We told her right away. But she was very upset and it took her a long time to become comfortable with it. She's twenty-one now."

Donna's husband, John, took over. "Maybe I knew all along about Kip. Some things made me wonder when he was growing up—not anything major, just little things. But you deny it. And I had never known a homosexual. For both Donna and me, our own son is the first one we've known. We've worked hard to understand this. He's said several times how important it is to him that we've accepted him and supported him. He's told us that many of his friends are in the closet with their families, having to hide something that is an integral part of who they are, or they've been rejected by their families after coming out to them."

"We worry about him getting AIDS, but he assures us that he's very careful," Donna added. "When he was in high school he dated a little and the girls just loved him. Gay guys don't hit on the girls and they appreciate that. He was very affectionate but didn't push them for a sexual relationship. The girls saw a guy who would respect them and be a wonderful companion. I told him, 'Women would *kill* for that kind of relationship.'

"Last Christmas he brought home Ron, whom he had dated quite a while. They've since broken up. Kip says it's hard for gay men to think about long-term relationships, because they don't have many role models. He says he knows one couple who have been together eight years and their relationship is rocky. Anyway, he brought Ron home, and I insisted that they have separate bedrooms, because that would be my rule with our daughter, too, and I decided they should be treated just the same. Kip had no problem with that."

"But they *were* affectionate with each other, and that was tough for me," John interjected. "I was shocked when I saw them kissing, hugging, and holding hands. I guess I knew they did it, but I couldn't get comfortable with that."

"I read everything I could find—everything *positive* I could find, that is, because I couldn't handle anything negative—and I got real sensitive to all the things homosexuals must go through," Donna said. "While Kip was in college I was ready to communicate my head off. I wanted to talk talk talk to him about this, but he wasn't ready for all that. I tried to rush him. I had to learn to wait until he was ready to talk about certain things. Right now he doesn't have a partner, but if he did and he wanted a religious ceremony, we'd certainly be there. We have friends who know about him and they would be there, too. We told Kip that we don't understand all of this, but we love him. He's our son. And we're going to support him."

"My story is a little bit like that," commented Eleanor, who had gotten to be good friends with Donna because of the support group. "In the beginning, when I thought about my son being gay, which I've known for three years now, I would feel like vomiting. I was raised to be accepting of people who are different, but I didn't know anything about homosexuals before I found out my son is one.

"I worry about his safety all the time. He and Phil, his partner, live in Minneapolis and they own a house. I know there have been incidents of violence in their area. I also worry about AIDS. I try not to think about it, but I'm afraid I'm always thinking about it. If he ever seems even slightly under the weather with a little cold or something, I get very agitated and can't sleep.

"Sam told me that he thought he'd always known he was gay. Maybe I did too and just didn't want to see it. I tried a million times to think what his father or I did to cause this and I can't come up with anything. Sam never did like sports like his brother did. He was interested in the arts—he's an artist—and he always liked clothes and played with girls. He actually dated a little bit in high school, but never much.

"He called me and told me on the phone because he said he thought I should know and he just couldn't look me in the eye and tell me. I'm glad his father didn't know before his death. It would have been so hard on him. It's hard on me, too. I've shed many, many tears over this and wished a million times that I could change it and Sam could be a family man. But I know that he and Phil *are* a family. Sam's sister and brother accept him, and their children love Sam and Phil. I guess they're learning that there are different kinds of families in this world.

"Not long ago I got a thank-you note from Phil for a gift I'd given him and he wrote me that he and Sam were very happy. 'We have everything we want and more than we need,' he said. And I thought, Gee, how many couples can say that? I don't cry anymore. I'm just so lucky to have such a wonderful son. And Phil is wonderful, too."

"This is my first time coming to this group," said Madge, who had listened attentively to these stories. "I'm not a parent. I'm here because my nephew Tony is dying of AIDS. He's in San Francisco and he's very sick and won't live long. He was born to my older sister when I was still in high school and he's always been like a son to me. I couldn't have children of my own, but I didn't mind because I had such a special relationship with Tony."

She began to cry, but she continued, her voice shaky. "I'm still trying to get used to all this," she said, apologizing. "We just found out a month ago that Tony had AIDS. This has all happened real fast. Tony is twenty-eight, a college graduate, and he had a very good job as an accountant. He hasn't been with another man for eight years, so he was probably HIV-positive for a long time. I didn't ask. He wants to come home to die, but he's so sick we may not get him here in time. I was with him in San Francisco last week and he's getting wonderful care there. The gay community really takes care of its own. They've had to because they've been so discriminated against and so many of them have no family contact.

"I had no idea Tony was gay until he turned eighteen and moved in with a male friend after he graduated from high school. He hid it perfectly. When he told the family, my brother-in-law was fine about it, but my sister demanded that Tony see a psychiatrist to get it 'fixed.' Tony went, but unfortunately it was a psychiatrist who told my sister Tony could change if he wanted to. Some psychiatrists and psychologists are still uninformed and they do a lot of damage to families. My sister took his word as gospel and she's been very unforgiving for what she says Tony has done to her. That's been real hard for him because he loves his mother. My sister is a good person, she just has her head in the sand.

"When I learned Tony was gay, I cried and cried and asked why it had to be him instead of someone else. He said, 'Aunt Madge, I wouldn't wish the hell I've gone through or what I'm going to go through on anyone.' I knew then that he couldn't change. But I was devastated.

"My husband has been wonderful about it. He said to me, 'Did he grow two heads? Has he committed murder? Has he done anything different than he's ever done?' I said no. 'Isn't he the same Tony we've always known and loved?' I had to say yes. And I thought, here's my husband, Mr. Macho Sports himself, and if he can accept this, I can learn to accept it, too.

"I started reading everything I could find, and I tried to pass along the best of things to my sister, but she wouldn't take them. I don't know what to do to help her. I know when Tony dies—and that will be soon—she's going to fall apart.

"Tony has two younger brothers, and I love them dearly, but Tony's always been so special. He never forgets a birthday or anniversary. He's very sensitive to people's feelings. And he's got a great sense of humor. I remember one night when I was cleaning closets—I'm a night owl—and Tony called me and asked what I was doing. When I told him, he said, 'Oh my God, I don't go near closets. It took me forever to get out of one.' We were able to laugh over little jokes like that.

"The AIDS connection with homosexuals is so unfair. Seventy percent of new cases are in heterosexuals. I sponsor our school's cheerleading squad, and given those girls' sexual behavior, I'm going to have a hard talk with them when school starts. They don't realize it can happen to them."

Madge began to cry again. As the group offered its comfort, Beverly Barbo, the chapter's founder and guiding light, said, "The people who come to this group are exceptional. They love their children and they're trying to understand what has happened to them and why. They are also willing to reach out and help anyone else they can. There's such an incredible need out there for comfort, support, and education. Homosexual young people are the only group who can't go home, can't share with anyone. They have no role models, no support systems. So many of them think they're the only ones in the world who feel the way they do. Their school counselors can't help them, and if they're the target of slurs or violence, the administration often won't do anything about it.

"We've got to start taking care of these children because they are killing themselves at a horrendous rate." Beverly's voice broke, but she went on. "I've heard so many horrible stories—of the young man whose father, a Baptist minister, stood over his hospital bed where he lay dying of AIDS and shouted, 'Hell is too good for you!' I met an Asian man whose family had actually held a 'killing ceremony' for him when they found out he was gay because he was the oldest son and they were 'eliminating' him from the family so the next-oldest son would inherit everything.

"My daughter teaches third grade and caught the kids playing Smear the Queer on the playground. Their victim was a sweet, thin little boy who will probably have to put up with that kind of thing all his life. When Pam questioned the children, they said, 'It's okay, teacher. Our folks say the only good queer is a dead queer.' We teach this hatred to our children. And if we find out a family member is gay, we turn against our own because we've been taught that this is what you must do.

"At the time our son Tim was dying of AIDS in a Los Angeles hospital in 1986, I got to know a young man who told me a chilling tale of walking down a street with two gay friends when they were suddenly surrounded by a gang whose initiation rite was to 'kill a queer.' This young man and one of his friends were beaten, tied up, and forced to watch while the third friend was brutally murdered and cut to pieces."

Beverly could barely tell this story, and while she brought herself under control, her husband, Dave, who runs a print shop in tiny Lindsborg, Kansas, continued. "Our son Tim had a rough life, and then, when he got AIDS, he went through horrible physical suffering. He was twenty-seven when he died.

"I grew up in a home where sex was never talked about. So did Beverly. We didn't talk about it to our three kids, either. Fortunately, our two surviving children are doing much better with their own kids. They know how important it is.

"Beverly always suspected Tim was gay, but I tried to ignore it. I guess I didn't want to admit I had a gay son. Tim came home from college his sophomore year and said, 'Dad, I'm a hopeless homosexual.' That's when Beverly and I finally accepted it. I wish we could have done this sooner so we could have helped him. We stumbled so many times. It's a tragedy we don't learn how to deal with differences in people."

Beverly took over. "Tim knew for sure he was homosexual when he was fifteen and had a crush on a senior boy. The other kids seemed to know, too, and made his life miserable. But unless it's said, it isn't so, and even though we were suspicious, we didn't talk about it. If we could have been open with our children about things pertaining to sex, perhaps Tim would have felt he could talk to us. But I didn't know anything about homosexuality, and Tim probably thought I was dumb, so why talk to me. We thought that with enough positive influence, if Tim had any choice in the matter, he'd make the right choice. Dave and I railed on and on about the immorality of homosexuality. We belonged to a fundamentalist church that taught this. Of course what we did was rip to pieces any self-esteem Tim had and make it all the tougher for him to come out to us. He was very unhappy growing up. He couldn't date, he had no chance to try out relationships and learn about them like other teenagers did. Alcoholism and drug abuse are rampant in the gay community to hide all this pain.

"When he finally came out to us, I immediately went to see our pastor. Let's just say he wasn't ready. Good Christian families shouldn't have this problem, he said, and maybe if we ignored it, it would go away. So we just kind of went on, and when it didn't go away, we tried to fix it. We went to psychologists and we prayed, and finally we had to face the fact that this wasn't something that could be fixed. We loved our son, our son was gay, and what we had to do was accept him for what he was and try to help him find his place in life.

"He tried college and eventually left and moved to San Francisco and got a good job. Later he moved to L.A. Those were the happiest years of his life. When he got to San Francisco, he found the gay community and he finally fit somewhere. It took a while before he and Tom found each other and settled in to a monogamous relationship. It was during that period of experimentation that we think Tim contracted AIDS and four years before he learned he had it. Had he found Tom sooner, they would probably both be alive.

"Tim and Tom were together over six years. Tom has since died of AIDS as well. The two of them were very happy together and very devoted to each other and we rejoiced that at last Tim had somebody to love and somebody to love him. We called Tom our son-in-love and we truly did love him like another son. Anyone who saw Tim and Tom together could see how much they loved each other and how right they were together. Our families were very accepting of them and included them in all family gatherings. I lived with Tim and Tom the last six months of Tim's life and saw their devotion to each other.

"I've had a lot of red burning rage at the church and I've had to work through that. It's as though we're not supposed to grieve for our son because of what he was. Because we've moved around a lot in our forty years of marriage, we've belonged to various congregations. We don't have any friends left in any of them. We stayed for two years after Tim died as burrs under the saddle of the church we were in at the time, but we finally had to leave. They've since had two other young men die of AIDS and they're not going to deal with it.

"As a society we've got to recognize gay couples as family. We've got to be open with our children, telling them that there are all kinds of families in this world.

"It's so sad when people can't show they love each other. As one soldier put on his gravestone, 'I got a medal for killing two men. I was discharged for loving one.' "

We returned to Kansas City as changed people. This loving group of parents, along with the Passages group, had heightened our sensitivity to homosexuality. We would never be neutral about it again.

What they taught us put one more piece of the puzzle into place for us. If we hadn't understood it before, we were understanding now of how basic love and sex are to life. Homosexual or heterosexual, we humans need emotional and physical intimacy. Engaging in sex is one form of touching, one form of gratification. Homosexuals receive that gratification from members of the same sex. The need is natural to them, and they can do nothing to change it. Our society's inability to accept and embrace that is a source of misery for our homosexual population and their families and friends.

In trying to educate the public about homosexuality, Beverly and Dave Barbo have been both embraced and vilified. They have been ostracized and called names, but they are indefatigable and will continue their crusade.

We had asked the group what advice they have for parents who suspect their children might be homosexual, or whose children have revealed this to them. We culled this list from what they said:

▶ Don't take it personally. You didn't do anything wrong, you didn't cause this. Most important, your child isn't *doing* this to you. Homosexuals do not *choose* their sexual orientation.

▶ Don't try to change them or insist they change themselves. It won't do any good and it could be harmful. Whatever you do, don't reject your child.

▶ Give yourself time to accept this. You need to work through any anger you may have as well as the grief you will experience for what will never be. You may need to confront your own homophobia—and this may require professional help.

▶ Welcome your children's friends and try to be accepting of a special friend. Your gay child should live by the same house rules as your other children.

▶ Educate yourself about homosexuality and help your child become educated about the realities they may have to face: How to protect themselves against violence, what health precautions they must take, what legal rights they do and do not have.

▶ Be loving, open, and accepting. Be very patient. It may take a long time before your children can be loving, open, and accepting of themselves, and they need your support very badly. You won't regret giving it.

▶ Seek out and find support groups. (See Appendix C at the end of this book.) Other parents who have faced this dilemma can be very helpful to you.

▶ If you can't find a support group in your area, start one. In giving others support, you will in turn receive it.

Judith Dutton, a psychotherapist in the Kansas City area whose expertise includes gay and lesbian issues, offered us some additional considerations for parents to think about.

"If parents can get through their own sense of failure about having a homosexual child, they still need to be cautious about the messages they give that child," she said from her office in Lawrence.

"You may love that child very much and give him or her all the support you can, but if in the process you say something like, 'Don't tell Grandma about this,' the message coming through to the child is that you're ashamed of their homosexuality.

"Adult homosexuals who adjust the best come from stable homes where their parents accept them for what they are and love them unconditionally. The gay man or lesbian who does not get that will always struggle at some level. In other words, the parents' acceptance is critical to the child's well-being."

Dutton believes more people are bisexual than we realize. "They face an incredible struggle, because the sexual desire is there for either sex, and most of them will try to settle into a monogamous relationship, usually with an opposite-sex member, since that's socially acceptable. While lesbians and gay men have their own supportive communities, bisexuals have no community to belong to.

"Bisexuality is not well documented," she said, "but I know from my practice that it's fairly common. Some bisexuals never make peace with who they are, going back and forth from gender to gender and never finding happiness."

Dutton recommends that parents of adolescents and young adults who are struggling with their sexual orientation seek peer support in groups like P-FLAG.

"As you work through your own struggles, be open to your children, and assist them in finding resources and, if necessary, professional help to learn to accept themselves. Be certain you interview the professional first to determine whether he or she sees homosexuality as a valid way of living and has experience in helping families work through this issue.

"You may find yourself grieving for what your child will never be—for the lost hopes and dreams. Your child may also grieve for these same things, but mostly your child will feel relief to finally be able to get on with accepting what he or she is. To live in this homophobic society, your child needs to be very strong and needs your unconditional love."

Too many parents go into the closet when their child comes out of it. They don't want family, friends, and neighbors to know. They hide it from church members and coworkers. They clothe themselves in shame and fear.

What we human beings must come to realize is that whatever one's sexual orientation may be, it's normal. We must overcome our fear and hatred of anything out of the mainstream. When we condemn people who are different, we may be condemning our own children.

Beverly Barbo said it best, bringing tears to the eyes of that group who met in a church in Salina, Kansas, on a hot summer afternoon.

"Our gay children are told there's something wrong with them," she said. "They are discriminated against, harassed, beaten, and sometimes even killed because of who they are. This isn't right. We must stand up for them. We must help people understand that we're all in the human condition together and that each one of us has worth.

"If we will do that, we will help to make the world a better place for our gay children, our gay grandchildren, and anybody else who happens for whatever reason to be a little different."

CHAPTER 7

WHEN THE ISSUE IS PREGNANCY

We had just gotten off the phone with Alex on a muggy Sunday morning in July, and we were feeling good as we sat down to have a second cup of coffee.

Alex had a new male "interest"! Or at least we hoped she did. She had talked about the Boyfriend, who apparently was still giving some thought to coming to visit her, but she also mentioned a new "friend" named Clay, and our hopes were high.

We had told her about our trip to Salina, trying to make her understand what an emotional and enlightening experience it had been for us. "That's interesting," she said. "People have the right to be whatever they are. It doesn't bother me." Then she changed the subject. She is like so many of us, in that her neutrality doesn't do enough to counteract the homophobic paranoia in our society. How can people understand the impact of homosexuality in a family unless they have experienced it at first hand or have attentively listened to those who have?

While we were musing on all this, the doorbell rang. Alex's girl-friend Susan was standing on the porch—in a maternity smock. We tried not to look surprised. We hadn't seen much of Susan since she had spent some time in a drug rehab program when she was fifteen, and she and Alex didn't see much of each other anymore. We had always enjoyed Susan's friendliness and wit.

We told her Alex was away for a few weeks. Seeing her disappointment and because it was so hot, we invited her in for a cool drink. We sat down at the kitchen table and offered her something to eat.

"I'd probably get sick," she said with a smile. "I can't eat in the mornings, just the afternoons. And sometimes I throw up my dinner."

"How far along are you?" we ventured, glad she had acknowledged the pregnancy.

"Almost seven months. I'm big, aren't I?" She grinned, her hands stroking her belly. "My mom threw up with all three of us until she was eight months along. I guess I'm the same."

"And do you plan to . . ."

"Keep the baby?" she guessed. "You bet! I'm real excited about it. I've got everything all planned. I want it to be a girl and she's going to have three names. I'm going to live with my friend Rhonda, who has a baby, and she'll take care of my baby while I go to school." She made a face. "I'm going to have to pump milk. Gross."

"Is Rhonda someone you've known a long time?"

She must have seen the concern in our eyes. "You're afraid she's one of my druggie friends, aren't you. I'm not doing that anymore I quit when I learned I was pregnant."

"Sorry," we murmured. "We don't mean to be nosy."

"It's okay. Hey, if you want, I'll tell you all about everything. You want me to? I don't mind, honest."

We nodded and settled in with our coffee while Susan talked.

"I'm kinda worried about all the drugs I was taking at the time I got pregnant, but my doctor keeps telling me he thinks I'll be okay and carry to full term. I was smoking a lot of pot and I'd discovered

pills. I *love* pills, especially Valium. My boyfriend Bobby was doing
a lot of drugs, too. That's how we got together. Some nights we'd
smoke a quarter bag of dope, which is a lot. It got me stoned, but it
was a brain-dead kind of feeling.

"I liked Bobby for things other than the drugs. It's my nature to
take care of people, and it started out with me taking care of him
because he has so many problems to deal with. He's never known his
father, and his mother is a real loser. He started abusing me for a
while, but we got it worked out. The sex was like, wow! It was great.
It was fun. We had feelings for each other.

"We didn't use any kind of birth control. I know we should have,
but I thought if you were on drugs you couldn't get pregnant. Maybe
I didn't really believe that, but, I don't know, we didn't *think* about
this happening. We just did what we wanted. Our attitude was, 'Who
cares?' We both had been with other people and it hadn't happened,
even though neither of us used anything.

"Anyway, we aren't together now. He's back in detox and I don't
want him on the birth certificate so there won't ever be any custody
fights. Rhonda says he still has to pay me support. Of course, he
doesn't have a job, but maybe he'll straighten up. He's going to have
to if he wants to spend time with the baby.

"I don't see myself with him. Maybe way in the future. He has
to prove himself. He has a lot of problems and he's just nineteen. I
really care about him, but he's a drug addict and I'm his only support.
I'm the only clean person in his life.

"I'm going to stay clean because of the baby. Before I got pregnant
my life was worthless. I just didn't give a crap. Now I've got a future.
I've signed up for all these programs so that my medical care and my
apartment and everything I need for the baby is all paid for. It won't
even cost me anything to go to college and I'm definitely going
to go.

"Before you ask, I *didn't* think about getting an abortion. Well,

I *thought* about it, but I think it's morally wrong. And I couldn't handle it at all to have the baby adopted by someone.

"Having a baby will be okay. It doesn't mean I have to stop having fun. I'm not going to be able to run out the door with my friends, but I already can't do that. Rhonda doesn't like having to stay home with her kid all the time, but she can go out when it's older.

"Me and my mom don't get along at all. We're too much alike. I'm living with her right now so I can get my medical card, but then I'm either going to go live at my dad's or with my grandma and then I'm moving into a home for unwed mothers so I can get my emancipated minor status and then collect welfare and move in with Rhonda. Since my mom and dad split up last year, they both have a lot on their minds, and I don't want to live with either of them. They don't have any room for me and a baby anyway, and I don't want my younger brother and sister around because they always get into my stuff.

"My mom figured out I was pregnant because I was throwing up a lot and sleeping all the time and she pestered me about when I'd had my period. When I finally said it'd been a long time, she made me go get tested. Mom's going to be my Lamaze partner because I can count on her.

"I actually started having sex a lot later than my friends. I didn't start until tenth grade. Everyone I knew had done it by eighth grade. I only know about two virgins and I'm not sure about one of them.

"I don't blame my parents for my drug problems or that I'm pregnant. I knew about birth control. I've always been wild and wanted to go out and experience everything. But not pregnancy. That was just stupid of me. I'm too young. I'm not going to have any more kids, at least not for a long time. I'm not going to date. I might get AIDS and I don't want to die and leave a baby behind. I worry about AIDS, even though most kids don't give it a thought.

"I'd like to get married someday, but I don't know. Maybe I'll just live with someone. Marriage is only a piece of paper anyway, and there aren't many nice guys out there, at least not the guys I see in my future.

"My friends are all stupid or fried. They still try to get me to do crazy things with them. They're completely unmotivated, they sit around and get high, and that's all they think about.

"One thing I know is, I'm going to teach my kid differently than I was taught. I'm going to try to be as honest as possible about sex and start right off talking *to* my kid, not *at* my kid. I'm watching adults with their kids to see what I think they do right and what they do wrong. I want to be a good mother."

She got a big grin on her face. "Boy, that's going to be strange having someone call me Mom. Cool!"

Five minutes after Susan left, her mother, Ellen, called, looking for her. We said Susan had just left and had told us she planned to stop at her dad's before she came home.

Ellen sighed. "She goes over there to get away from me so we won't fight. I'll be relieved when she moves out." She paused. "You do know she's pregnant, right?"

We put Ellen on the telephone's speaker so we could both talk to her. We told her we were concerned about Susan, but that she seemed to have everything thought out and under control.

"Well, I don't know what option there is to the way things are working out," Ellen said with a voice full of weariness. "Susan is headstrong and she's going to do what she wants to do. It's always been that way with her."

As we talked, we began to get a different side to the story of Susan. Ellen was clearly worried about her.

"I try to help her," Ellen said. "I'm the one who makes her doctor appointments and makes sure she takes her vitamins. I'm the practical one.

"She seems to be taking care of herself physically, but she's a mess psychologically. I know she doesn't feel good about herself or her life, but I don't know how to help her. When we're together, all we do is fight. You can't tell her anything.

"She's always been a secretive, difficult child, and now here's a new generation. I worry about the baby. I worry that Susan will go back to drugs. She doesn't know what she's in for. She has no idea how much work a baby is. She wants to be grown up and be treated like an adult and she thinks this is the answer. But what adults see is a child with a child. I truly believe, though, that if she somehow lost the baby, she would immediately get pregnant again.

"I taught her about birth control. I even gave her condoms. These kids today are all having sex. You can't stop them. I think she's been sexually active for a long time, but I don't know.

"I hope the baby's a girl because it's going to be raised in a female household. Probably by a mother who hasn't even graduated from high school. It'll take Susan at least two more years full-time to graduate, and I'm afraid she'll quit. She doesn't like to work. She's always quit any job she's had. She knows with welfare she'll have about as much money as if she worked. She doesn't like to get up in the morning, and if you're getting a welfare check you don't have to get up. I'm not even sure how she'll get herself up at night to feed the baby.

"My big fear is that I'll end up with the baby. Since the divorce, I'm just starting to get my life on track and I don't want that. It's my time now," she concluded, her voice full of resentment. "I don't want to start over with a baby."

We sympathized, expressing our concern for all of the family. We also registered our protest that in Kansas the taxpayers were picking up the tab for everything for Susan and the baby. Ellen passed right over that, so we didn't pursue it. But when the conversation ended, we found ourselves with mixed feelings about all that financial aid Susan would receive—especially the opportunity for a free college education under a new Kansas program. Too many middle-class parents, ourselves included, were wondering how to pay for our children's higher education. Some teenage girls might get the message, "If you want a college education, have a baby and the state will pay for everything." At the same time, we shared Ellen's concern that the baby get what it needed and not be jeopardized because it had a teenage parent.

But what is the best solution when teenage girls get pregnant— and marriage or single parenthood isn't a viable option?

This had been a concern for us when we faced the possibility that Alex might be pregnant. Thank God she wasn't, but she could have been. What would she have done? Clearly marriage to the Boyfriend was *not* the right solution. But was raising a baby on her own better?

Only two other choices existed: abortion and adoption. Both were fraught with emotional land mines.

Which decision is right for whom?

To pursue this issue a little further, we contacted a counselor who had organized and now facilitates a support group for teenage girls who have had abortions and asked if we could talk to several of them.

Three agreed to visit with us, and we met the first two at the counselor's office. The counselor told us the third girl was willing to see us later, and then closed the office door and left us alone with Tawna, sixteen, and Kerry, seventeen.

Chances are Tawna and Kerry would not have been friends if they were not in the same support group, even though they attend the same suburban high school. Tawna is from a working-class family. Kerry's father is a lawyer. She was dressed more expensively and was better groomed than Tawna. But they were closely linked because both had experienced abortions.

Tawna's abortion had taken place two years earlier during the summer before her freshman year. Kerry's had been in the spring, just three months ago. Both girls were willing to answer any question we asked.

Kerry spoke first, barely looking at us. Her voice was always soft, forcing us to listen carefully.

"I tried to pretend I wasn't pregnant and I didn't do anything about it until I was over five months along. By then I was starting to show and I knew I couldn't hide it any longer. I had already told my boyfriend, Randy, right when I first missed my period. I thought he would want me to have the baby. Instead he said it wasn't his and walked away from me.

"I was so broken up. I thought he loved me. He always said he did whenever we—you know—did it. We did it a lot. Sometimes we used condoms, but neither of us liked them, so sometimes we didn't.

"After he said that to me I knew I had to make a decision by myself. I was so confused. I thought maybe he'd change his mind, so I tried to talk to him and all he said was get an abortion.

"I finally told a friend that I thought I was pregnant and didn't know what to do. She helped me set up an appointment at a clinic for an abortion on practically the last day I could get one because I was getting so far along.

"They told me it was going to take two full days—counseling on the first day, and then they put these things inside you so you start to dilate, and then the next day they do the abortion. I couldn't figure out how to keep it from my parents, so the night before I told them. I just sort of blurted it out when we were finishing dinner. We don't usually eat together, but my dad was home that night, so I just said it. He got real angry and upset and kept insisting I tell him who the father was, but I refused. I'd never brought Randy over to the house, so they didn't know about him.

"See, I hate my parents. I hate the life they lead—it's all centered around their country club and going out to dinner with friends and money and stuff. Randy's got a ponytail and wears an earring. I didn't want my parents to meet him because then they would have ragged on me to drop him.

"Anyway, my dad yelled and screamed and my mom and I cried and they asked me what I was going to do and I told them I was getting an abortion the next day. My mom said she would go with me. She did—she sat in the waiting room the whole two days—but they never talked to me about it, even though I had a lot of problems afterward and had to go in for a D&C. It was like, Okay, that's over. Get on with life."

"My mom's the complete opposite," Tawna said. "I was stupid to get pregnant. Me and Ray weren't using anything because I didn't want to. My mom keeps track of my periods and she knew I hadn't started mine, so I'd only missed one when she brought up the subject and said I better get tested. When the test was positive, she made the appointment for me the next day. We never discussed it or anything. So I didn't even think about it, I just did it. My mom's had at least one, so she could have talked to me about it. It doesn't really bother me like it does other people. Maybe because it all happened so fast that I didn't get attached or anything."

"That's the difference," Kerry said. "I could feel the baby kicking. And they told me at the clinic that it was a girl and that's what I wanted."

"I'm still with Ray," Tawna continued. "I figure we'll get married. He dropped out last year and he has a pretty good job. He didn't try to stop the abortion. He was real supportive. Me and mom didn't tell my stepfather. I don't know my real father. He left before I was born.

But my stepfather has a temper and he would have killed Ray. He knows we have sex, because he caught us once in my bedroom and he got so mad he went to the garage to get his gun and Mom had to lock him out of the house until he cooled down. So we knew we couldn't tell him.

"I'm not glad I got pregnant, but I'm glad I got the abortion. I have a friend who has a baby and it's pretty bad. She never gets to do anything and the baby cries all the time. Sometimes I'm worried about how much she slaps the kid. I don't think it's good. I wouldn't want to do that to a kid because it's not the kid's fault. So I think abortion is better."

"I guess I also felt worse because I really wanted to keep the baby," Kerry said. "And the abortion was so hard. I was so far along and it hurt so bad. Right now I don't think I made the right decision.

"I'm on the birth-control pill now because the clinic put me on it, but there's no way I could have gotten birth control before through my parents. They would have demanded to know who I was doing it with, and they would have yelled at me. The first few months I had a hard time with the pill, but I guess I'll probably always be on it now because guys hate condoms. I know you're still supposed to use them because of diseases and all, but I don't know anybody with a disease, so I guess I'll take my chances. Besides, it's just too hard to ask a guy to use one. Usually you don't know him well enough. And if you carry them, then he thinks you're a slut."

"When you really love someone, asking him to use condoms is like saying, 'I don't trust you,' " Tawna said. "I'd used condoms before with other guys, but they're like this barrier between you. So now I'm on the pill, too. No more condoms."

Kerry's voice cracked with emotion when she continued. "The worst thing that happened to me was, after I'd had the abortion, my ex-boyfriend came up to me and said, 'You killed my baby. If you'd loved me, you'd have kept it.' Can you believe it? First he denied it was his, then he told me to get an abortion, and then he said that. I was hysterical.

"I wish my parents would have taught me better. My mom told me about my period and that was it. For the rest of it, I had to experiment. The only thing my parents said about sex was not to do it. My dad once told me if he ever caught me with a guy he'd kill him. Parents have to accept that we have sex. We all do. I started in eighth grade and I've been with—I don't know, several guys. If my parents had been more open about it, I wouldn't have been five months along before I did something about it.

"If I ever get pregnant again, I'm keeping the baby. I wouldn't care if the guy left or stayed. If my parents didn't want to be part of my life, it wouldn't matter to me."

Her big green eyes filled with tears. "I should have done what I wanted. I should have said I love this baby and I'm going to keep it and I don't care. I may have kids someday, but it's going to be so hard knowing I don't have as many as I could have had."

Tawna putting a comforting arm around her. "I don't know what I'd do if I got pregnant again," Tawna said. "I'm going to try not to, but if I did, well, I don't know. I wouldn't let it be adopted because I couldn't give away my own kid. So I guess I'd have another abortion.

"I started my period in fourth grade and it was really embarrassing. I started doing it with guys by the time I was twelve. It's pretty bad out there. I don't know anybody who doesn't do it. They make fun of you as long as you're a virgin. I used condoms or the guy pulled out, but I felt really trashy because I didn't care for any of them. The first time was just to get it over with and it was painful. I wish my first time could have been with Ray because I was his first time and it bothers him.

"But I don't know if you should wait too long to start having sex because I know this girl who waited until she was seventeen and she got pregnant the first time. She had an abortion and now she's doing it with all these guys. I think she's just trying to make up for what she thinks she's missed."

Later we visited with Jade. Like Kerry, she was seventeen. She's a pretty girl, nicely dressed, with blue eyes, a light dusting of freckles, and deep auburn hair.

"This all happened last fall," she said in a husky voice. "I knew I was pregnant the first month because my period is so regular. I was sixteen then and I'd been going with my boyfriend Dave for about ten months. We've been together about a year and a half now. We started having sex after the first week we met and we used birth control. I was on the pill, but I was really terrible about remembering to take it, so we also used condoms."

She looked momentarily embarrassed. "We use those because we both have herpes.

"Anyway, the week I got pregnant I'd been forgetting to take the pill and we'd had a couple of condoms break, so I guess that was the problem. When we found out I was pregnant, we decided to keep it. We had that dream of being a happy married couple with a cute baby. But then we started thinking, We're going to have to work too hard. We're not ready for this. I didn't want to end up blaming the baby if my life got screwed up.

"I'm probably lucky I hadn't gotten pregnant before, because I've been having sex since I was twelve. My first time was with this neighbor guy who was fourteen. It just kind of happened. You know how it is, you welcome new experiences. I just wanted to try it and I didn't stop him when he got started. Dave was eleven when he started. I've had a medium amount of partners, maybe ten. Dave is about the same. But this is the most intense relationship either of us has had.

"It stalled for a while after the abortion. Sex wasn't good anymore.

It got routine, I guess, and didn't mean anything. We got mad at each other for every little thing. So we stopped having sex. We'd talk about it—in fact, we talked about it all the time—but we didn't do it. I don't know how long we lasted, but several months. Then when we started again it was real good. Maybe the problem was we both started having sex so young. When we did it again, it was sort of like the first time and it was much nicer.

"My mom put me on the pill at thirteen because she knew I was having sex and she couldn't stop me. She was always nervous that something would happen. She never said sex that young was wrong, but I knew she thought it was. I know my fourteen-year-old brother is doing it, because I caught him and his girlfriend when they were both thirteen. I gave him rubbers and I had a talk with her and I think they're being careful.

"I got herpes from my boyfriend before Dave. By the time I had my first breakout and told Dave, I'd already given it to him. He gets outbreaks more often than I do and he gets real mad at me. There's no cure. It could do bad stuff to a baby. You have to be careful and probably have a C-section.

"Anyway, when I got pregnant Dave said he'd support whatever I wanted to do. It was a hard decision, because by then I was three months along and getting pretty attached. I'd told my parents I was pregnant and they wanted me to have an abortion. But just to make things okay, everybody went to counseling—my folks, my boyfriend, his parents, and me. We went together and separately and all that. I agreed to listen to everybody's opinion, but the agreement was that it was my decision. I know my parents—my mother, that is—wanted to tell me what to do, but I wasn't going to allow that.

"After I made my decision, my parents arranged the abortion. It cost $500, and Dave paid part of it. My dad and Dave took me to the clinic. My mom had to be out of town on business for a few days. Afterward I didn't feel too good and I just wanted to rest at home.

Dave was with me. But my dad just sort of went crazy that night. It was real hot and muggy outside for some reason, and I was pleading with him to turn on the air conditioning and he wouldn't do it. He started calling me all these terrible names—really gross, dirty things—and getting all mad at Dave. He was a real asshole, a real nightmare.

"I was hot and dizzy and nauseated. I had so much pain. I thought I was going to die. My dad kept pushing me down on the couch when I tried to get away from him and he was screaming at me and screaming at Dave. I was afraid they'd hit each other. Dave refused to leave because my father was being so awful. I've never forgiven him for that night. I still barely speak to him.

"Now I have the Norplant implant in my arm. See?" She held up her arm, pressing in on the flesh to show the outline of the matchstick implants. "I think it's the greatest. No pregnancy worries for five years!"

She got a faraway look in her eyes. "Someday when I'm an adult and I'm ready, I'll have kids. I think whether or not to have the baby should be the girl's choice. I mean, I wouldn't have been any kind of mother. I'm too young. I'm still a child. I really love Dave, but I would have lost him if I'd had the baby because we weren't ready to raise a child together. I'm real lucky my parents and Dave supported me. It's so tough, even with support. I don't know how anybody gets through it without that."

Did these girls make the best decision for themselves? *Is* there a best decision when a teenage girl gets pregnant?

Susan will be part of the 97 to 98 percent of unwed mothers in this country who keep their babies, and she will find out how difficult it is to raise a baby alone. Tawna, Kerry, and Jade have learned how difficult abortion is. They are part of the half-million teenage girls in this country whose pregnancies end every year in abortion or miscarriage. With various state legislatures enacting legislation such as the new law in Kansas requiring consent from at least one parent or else permission from a judge, that number may go down, or it may mean that more teens will seek illegal abortions.

It remains to be seen whether it means more teens will choose to "adopt out."Because of access to birth control and abortion, and society's changing views of unwed mothers, only a small percentage of pregnant teenagers make that choice. But just a couple of decades ago, giving birth out of wedlock was so shameful that well-meaning families would sometimes send their pregnant daughters to the maternity homes that thrived in places like Kansas City. The girl usually had little or no say in what was happening to her. She was brought to the home, delivered her baby there, and left without it. Rarely was she asked what she wanted to do or given any option. The babies were put up for adoption.

Happily for couples trying to adopt, some girls still do adopt out. For many reasons it's the most difficult of the options open to a pregnant teenager. To find out what it was like, we called the LIGHT-house in Kansas City, a nondenominational Christian care center for pregnant teenagers. The majority of the girls who reside there plan to keep their babies. A few place their babies for adoption.

We talked to a social worker who arranged for us to visit with fifteen-year-old Erin and eighteen-year-old Davina, both of whom were pregnant and planning to adopt out. We visited with Erin first, meeting her in the cheerful "parents' room" at the center.

Erin comes from a small town north of Kansas City. She's a pretty blond, shy and soft-spoken. When we visited with her she was four months pregnant.

"I thought about keeping my baby, but I'm only fifteen and I don't have any way to take care of it or support it," Erin said, her voice hesitant. "My dad wanted me to get an abortion, but my mom

got real religious a few years ago and said that was wrong and I should
have it. I think she's right, because this isn't the baby's fault.

"My boyfriend—make that my *ex*-boyfriend—didn't want abortion either, but he also didn't want a kid. He's twenty-one. We didn't
use any birth control. I thought it was my safe time of the month.
Besides, I hadn't gotten pregnant before when I'd had sex. He didn't
really pressure me to have sex, but I was afraid I'd lose him. I guess
I didn't know him well enough to discuss something like birth control.

"I don't know how many girls he's been with. Probably a lot. He
was only the second guy I've really loved. I met him at the park and
I really liked him right away. Even though he said he loved me, I
guess it didn't mean anything to him. It was just a line.

"I moved to my town when I was thirteen and I couldn't believe
how many kids there were having sex. By eighth grade they'd all done
it. The girls want it as much as the boys. Everybody says things like,
'I want to get laid this weekend.' Girls have to be kind of careful or
they get bad reputations. The guys are cool, the girls are sluts—that
sort of thing. The girls say it about other girls as much as the
guys do.

"There's a health clinic in town, and that's where the girls go to
get the pill or condoms. If you don't have a job, they're free or real
cheap. It's easy to get them, but I never did. I started having sex when
I was fourteen and I just didn't figure anything would ever happen.
I've had sex with three different guys—not nearly as many as most
girls I know.

"My mom thinks I had sex to punish her for something, but I
wasn't even thinking about her. I did it because I had feelings for my
boyfriend. Afterward I was happy. But now I feel used. I'm just one
more girl to him. He got what he wanted and now he's in California
and I don't know if I'll see him again.

"If I have another boyfriend, I'm going to see how he treats his mother because they say you can tell from that how he'll treat his wife. My boyfriend was really mean to his mom. He wasn't mean to me, except he disappeared after I got pregnant. My mom says that's what guys always do.

"I feel awful alone, except that my mom's been pretty good about coming to visit. She says it'll be hard knowing there's a child out there she's related to. She's going to be with me when the baby's born. I asked her if she was going to hold it and she started to cry. This experience has definitely made us closer. I'm more open with her and we can talk about so many more things now. I can't deny anything because everyone knows I had sex. I'm really sorry I disappointed my mom so much.

"My dad is real embarrassed, since everybody in town knows where I am. He's a businessman and he thinks this will ruin his reputation. He said terrible things to me. He blamed me and called me names. He kept using the "f" word and calling me a whore and it really hurt me a lot. He doesn't want me to come home on weekends because he's afraid people will see me.

"I wish he hadn't called me those names. The rest of it I can handle. I'll get through it. I know I've made a mess of things and I'm really sorry, but I'm trying to make the best of it.

"It will be hard to tell another guy about all this. He might not understand or he might think it was wrong of me to give up the baby. But I guess if a guy really loves you he can accept anything you've done.

"The movies make sex look so good and they make it look like you don't have to worry about birth control. They don't show the bad side of sex. They don't show girls getting hurt. We see the movies and then we do it. There's a fourteen-year-old here who has a twenty-six-year-old boyfriend and she thinks he's going to stick by her once she has the baby. I bet he leaves.

"Nobody thinks about STDs or AIDS. I guess we have a couple

of kids in our school who are HIV-positive. That's what you hear. I don't know if it's true. Once in a while you hear 'So-and-so's got the crabs' but not very often. Parents should know that they've got to talk to their kids earlier. Eighth grade's too late. They need to start by fifth grade. Sex is just a part of life and it happens all the time.

"It's going to be hard giving up the baby. I've already bonded to it. Abortion would have been the easy way out, and giving up your baby is a lot harder than keeping it. What keeps me going is that at least I know I can have children, and there are people out there who can't who would love to have a child. I don't need one right now. That doesn't mean I don't love it. I hope more than anything my child will know I loved it and wanted the best for it, and that's why I gave it to good people to raise."

Erin left and the social worker who had invited us to the LIGHT-house came in to visit with us while we waited for Davina, who was also going to visit with us.

"Erin's been through a real struggle," she said. "She's more mature than most girls. She's actually thought about what it's going to be like to see her baby for the first time and then give it up. She knows how hard it's going to be.

"We place about twenty-five to thirty babies a year. Our waiting list of parents averages three years in length.

"At any given time we will have anywhere from ten to forty girls here. They come from every race and social class, and they come from all over the country and even foreign countries. We're pro-life, so abortion is not an option for them. We keep our costs very low in order to encourage the girls not to have abortions. They either plan to keep their babies, they adopt out, or they aren't sure and need some time to decide between the two. Some of them know what they're going to do but are having problems at home and just need a cooling-off period, so they stay here awhile.

"We're considered a homeless shelter by the state and a girl will automatically qualify for Medicaid unless she has independent income, like a trust fund. We have different ways to help the parents and the girl deal with medical expenses.

"One of our goals is to help teenage mothers have healthy babies and to help both mother and baby get off to a good start. We make sure all the girls get good nutrition, medical care, plenty of rest, and appropriate education. We also offer support after the birth, whether or not the girl has kept the baby. The girls know there's always a counselor here they can talk to.

"Some of the girls who have been raised by single parents think that's fine and are keeping their babies. Others have seen the struggle their single parent has been through and don't want to do that and plan to adopt out.

"Others, like Erin, think they've made a mistake and want to make the best of it. Most of the girls want their babies to have fathers, and in ninety-nine out of a hundred cases the father is usually out of the picture by the time a girl gets here. We have very few fathers who will even cooperate with the adoption. They don't cause any trouble, but they won't sign the papers. Because of Missouri law, that means the baby must be with a foster family for sixty days before it can go to its adoptive family. Important bonding time is lost. If the father will sign the papers, we can have the baby with its adoptive family within two weeks. If the mother refuses to name the father, we must also go the sixty-day route.

"Sometimes girls change their minds at the last minute and keep their babies. That seems to go through cycles, sometimes depending on what kind of peer support they get here. Surrendering the babies is extremely difficult, as you can imagine.

"When a pregnant girl wants to keep her baby, regardless of her age, the best thing her parents can do is tell her up front exactly what they will provide and what they won't—and then stick with it. It's important that she not get mixed messages from her parents.

"Even if a girl's parents are supportive of her keeping the baby, there can be lots of problems. Especially when the mother is very young, it's usually *her* mother who ends up taking care of the baby. Then when the girl wants control back, her mother has already bonded to the baby as her own and a real struggle can ensue."

Davina came in and the social worker left. Davina was eight months pregnant and as outgoing as Erin had been shy. A pretty brunette with a bubbly personality, she smiled a lot and was very open with us. She's from a small town in South Dakota and before coming to the LIGHThouse had been attending a South Dakota college on a basketball scholarship.

"My baby's due August 15 and I'm just hoping it'll be on time so I can get back to college the last week of August," Davina said. "My mom was at least ten days late with my younger sisters and me. I sure hope I'm not the same way.

"I was six months pregnant before I told my parents. I kept trying to deny that I was pregnant until finally it was becoming obvious. I was a freshman at college last year and it was my first time away from home.

"Just before I left for school last fall, I broke up with the boyfriend I'd had for four years. He was the only guy I'd ever had sex with. Toward the end it wasn't a healthy relationship. I was totally dependent upon him for everything. Our decision to break up was mutual. We both knew we needed to give it a rest.

"I met Darren my second or third day at school. I didn't know a soul. I went there because they gave me a basketball scholarship. Darren was a sophomore and a big-time football player. Everybody knew who he was. The athletic department had this mixer for all the athletes, and that's where we met. I'd come out of this little high school where I had seventy-five kids in my class, and he was this smooth-talking upperclassman. I guess I also must mention that he's black, and I was sort of intrigued by that since we didn't even have any blacks in my high school and I'd never personally known one before.

"We started going out and we had sex almost from the beginning. But we used protection. That's the bummer. I know girls who have slept with tons of guys without using anything, and I've slept with only two guys and used condoms and I'm pregnant.

"Darren's not my boyfriend anymore. I told him right away when I thought I might be pregnant, and he told me to get it taken care of. He never said, 'What are *we* gonna do?' It was always 'What are *you* gonna do?' By the time I told him definitely that I was, we'd split. He was seeing other girls and I just couldn't put up with that.

"At first I thought about keeping the baby, but I knew I'd have to give up my scholarship and quit college. I truly didn't want to do that. Getting the scholarship had been such a big thing, and my parents couldn't pay for my college without it. You know how sometimes you suspect a girl will end up a certain way? Well, this shouldn't have happened to me. I was too nice, too smart, too good an athlete.

"I thought I was in love with Darren or I wouldn't have had sex with him. My parents had always said don't have sex until you get married, but everybody I knew was doing it. My roommate, all the girls in the dorm. It just seemed like the natural thing to do.

"My parents said it went against them and against God. But I have my own values, not my parents', and I don't think God judges things like this. I didn't do this to spite my parents. This is *my* life. My mom thinks it's her fault, that she did something wrong, that maybe she and Dad fought too much or something. That's not true. I guess I knew I shouldn't do it, but I wanted to.

"The couple of times my parents tried to talk to me about sex, it was just too embarrassing." Davina began to laugh at the memory. "My dad tried one night when he and I were at a Pizza Hut. Can you believe that? And I remember my mom bringing it up one night at the dinner table. It was before I'd done it, so I didn't even listen because it didn't apply to me. Basically all she said was don't do it, but it was so embarrassing I wouldn't even talk to her.

"My parents don't know I had sex with my high school boyfriend. I wish I would have waited, because after a while my relationship with him was nothing but sex and it got to the point where it didn't mean anything. We didn't communicate and we fought all the time. With Darren, I wish I'd never done it at all.

"You know how it is—it's okay to have sex, but it's not okay to get caught. If you do, you're an outcast. I wish someone had taught me how to recognize a line when you're getting fed one, because that's what happened to me. Darren knew what to say to get what he wanted. I'd had sex education at school, but there wasn't anything about how sex was part of a relationship or how to protect yourself against rape or a smooth talker or anything like that.

"My high school girlfriends and I would always talk about how sex was part of a bigger relationship and we'd be with the guys we did it with forever. I know only one girl who's still with that boyfriend. Some of my friends started having sex at fourteen and I couldn't believe they were doing it. I waited until sixteen and I thought I was in love, and I never bragged about it to my friends.

"My little sister is sixteen and she's got a steady boyfriend. I need to talk to her. I don't think she's doing anything, but nobody thought I was either. She needs to know about the lines guys use and that sometimes birth control doesn't work. She probably thinks I wasn't using anything. Birth control is really up to the girl, because guys get so—urgent. They just have to do it. It doesn't have anything to do with love, they've just gotta have it and can't stop. They always say they'll pull out and then they don't. They always say at the time they love you, but they don't. They want sex, and the girl wants a boyfriend.

"I think this experience has made me grow up a lot. I've learned I can't depend on guys or they'll take advantage of me. Darren knows I'm here and I think he'll sign the papers. He knew keeping the baby wasn't the right thing, and I'd waited too long to get an abortion. I think that's why I refused to admit I was pregnant for so long—I didn't want anyone talking me into doing that.

"My parents found out when my mom called me on the day I had told my basketball coach that I was pregnant. I knew if I didn't tell him someone else would, because I wasn't going to be keeping it a secret much longer. Anyway, my mom could tell on the phone that I was really depressed and she kept asking me what was wrong. I just kept saying that it was the worst thing she could possibly think of. Finally she guessed and then I started to cry. She got real upset and yelled at me. She kept saying, 'How could you do this to us?' Then she put my dad on the phone, and he was real nice and supportive and said they'd help me get through it. I felt a lot better when I got off the phone.

"The funny thing is, my mom called later to apologize for getting upset, and then my dad went off the wall when he found out the father was black and started calling me all these ugly racist names. He kept referring to Darren as 'that nigger.' Not long ago he apologized for getting so upset and told me if I kept the baby he'd try to learn to love it even though it was part black. But he can't talk about Darren at all without getting real angry and using bad language.

"Dad's an electrician and he's had kind of a hard life and he really wanted me to get my education. I think he's glad I've made this decision and am going back to school in the fall. My mom found the LIGHThouse for me. Both my parents told me to do what was right for me, and I think this is best for both the baby and me. I'm not really crazy about little kids, so it's not like I'm dying to have a baby. Someday I want children, but not now. I want to finish my education and play some good ball and then maybe be a coach.

"If I kept this baby, we'll both be poor. I can't give this baby a good life and someone else can. It would be real hard to raise a mixed-race baby in my hometown and I would want to be there near my family. This way the baby can go to a family that doesn't mind mixed race and will raise it in a home and a town where that's more accepted.

"If I marry and have children, I'll tell them when they're older what I did. I think they have the right to know.

"I think my parents handled all this pretty well. They're supportive and I know they love me. What you need when you're in a situation like this is for your parents to be there for you and to not judge. It really helps.

"Some of the girls here talk about how they're going to make up for lost time once this is over. One girl my age is about to have her third child. She had her first one when she was thirteen. She kept the first two but is giving this one up. I think I have more values and goals than most of these girls.

"I'm not having sex again until I'm married. I know what I did isn't wrong—I just got caught—but it's not worth the risk. I'm bearing the responsibility, but I think girls always do. Guys can just leave. Being a guy is so easy."

We thought Erin and Davina were wise beyond their years. As they had said themselves, they were trying to make the best of bad situations. We wished them well with all our hearts and knew how grateful the families who adopted their children would be to them.

On the way home from the LIGHThouse we found ourselves talking about Davina's last line, about how guys could just leave and being a guy was so easy.

Was it? For some guys it might be, but for others, those raised by caring parents to be sensitive and loving, we knew that couldn't be the case. Boys seemed so overlooked in all this. Yes, we'd read about teenage and young adult males who indiscriminately father children by different mothers and have no intention of supporting them, but what's the other side of that story?

We remembered one parent we'd talked to telling us she had a close friend whose high-school-age son had fathered a baby out of wedlock and how difficult this had been for everyone concerned.

We called to ask if she thought the friend would visit with us, and soon we were in the friend Sonya's cheerful blue-and-white old farmhouse kitchen in one of the southeastern suburbs of Kansas City.

"My son Jason was such a good kid," she began, her face solemn. "Everybody in town watched him grow up and knew and liked him. He was in lots of activities, responsible, nice to his two younger brothers and us. We didn't have any complaints. And then during his sophomore year of high school, when he was sixteen, he began dating Jana, a senior girl who was new in school.

"Jason was absolutely smitten. He hadn't dated much and here was this beautiful, smart, *older* girl putting the moves on him. It's easy to see why he couldn't resist. He really went berserk.

"Jana's family was new in town and we didn't know them. Later we found out that they'd had lots of behavior problems with Jana and put her in a Catholic school hoping to get her straightened out. The family was strict with her in an odd sort of way. The parents aren't very involved with the children. They're cold and aloof. I think Jana craved affection and attention.

"Anyway, she set her sights on Jason, and everything happened so fast that they'd had sex before it even occurred to us that they might. They started dating in January and by March she was pregnant.

"The only message we'd given Jason about sex was don't do it. He'd always been so well behaved that we didn't worry. So by the time I finally talked to him about condoms, when it was clear how intense this relationship was, it was too late. I asked Jason if there was any possibility Jana was pregnant, because I noticed how tired and wan she looked. She had too many signs. He asked her but she said she wasn't. She denied it until May, and by then abortion was out of the question.

"Abortion would have been very difficult for us anyway, since we're Catholic, but so were her parents, and when they finally found out, they wanted her to get one. I believe now that she wanted to be pregnant, and if she'd had an abortion or miscarriage she would have just gotten pregnant again. She also wanted Jason, and as we've learned, she'd do anything to keep him.

"As the pregnancy progressed, our whole family went into counseling. We just couldn't talk to Jason. Things deteriorated so badly at home that he had to move in with my sister and her husband. All the conflict in our household was hurting us all. Jana moved into a private home because she couldn't get along with her parents either.

"Jason wanted to break up with her, but she kept threatening suicide, and he convinced himself that he loved her. He was very pleased when she agreed to give up the baby for adoption. He readily signed the adoption papers.

"Then at the last moment she decided to keep the baby. Her parents said she could live at home, but after a couple of months she got into a fight with them and they threw her out.

"Jason, of course, was the white knight. He helped her get set up in an apartment. She was out of high school and had a job, and Jason worked part-time while he finished high school. Then he moved in with her, and now he's in an emotionally abusive, destructive relationship. She constantly threatens suicide, and their poor little boy gets caught in the middle of it all.

"Jana's parents won't take care of the little boy. We have him quite a bit, and of course we've grown to love him very much. We even tried to go to court and get custody of him after Jason moved back home because his fights with Jana were getting so awful. She's a terrible mother, and it's possible we might have gotten custody, but she persuaded Jason to move back and try again, and that ended that.

"Jana was very angry at us for trying to get custody and told us she would make sure their little boy knows what 'bad people' we are.

When Jason is there, he's his little boy's primary care giver. He really loves him and takes good care of him.

"Now Jana is twenty-one, Jason is nineteen, and our grandson is two and a half. Jason and Jana plan to get married next year. He works full-time at a grocery store to support them and has never gotten to go to college. He knows he can always come home, that our house is open to him and we love him. I don't know what will happen. I don't believe a marriage between them can succeed. Jason is not happy, nor do I believe he still loves Jana, but he loves his son and feels he needs to stick in there for his child's sake.

"Teenagers think a problem like this affects only them, but it doesn't at all. It affects the whole family. My husband and I have continued to go to counseling because that helps us deal with the day-to-day stress of this situation, but it doesn't help with all the 'if only's' we torment ourselves with: If only we'd done this or that, maybe this wouldn't have happened.

"I do think the major mistake we made was in not teaching Jason about birth control. Jana wanted to get pregnant to get out of a bad family situation, so it would have been up to Jason. We've all got to face up to the fact that kids today are sexually active, even ones like Jason who were taught the difference between right and wrong.

"How can families counteract the media and the peer pressure? The principal at our high school believes that over 50 percent of the students are sexually active. Four senior girls in last year's class of fifty were pregnant. Who knows how many had abortions. Something has to be done. Kids today believe they have a green light to do whatever they want. They all think, 'It's not going to happen to me.'

"Teenage fathers get very short-changed in the system. Jason had no say-so in what would happen to that baby, and he has few legal rights. Boys have guilt feelings too, but everybody treats them like they're going to be deadbeats and refuse to support their children.

Anything positive focuses on the girl. Our loving, responsible sons shouldn't be pushed out of the picture or dismissed as bad people."

But few parents of daughters feel that way. We talked to another mother, Lois, whose daughter Emily got pregnant last year when she was fifteen. In sharp contrast to Sonya, Lois thinks boys have too many rights.

"He can take us to court. He gets the benefit of the doubt in everything," she said bitterly. "He doesn't have to pay a dime and he's never given the baby a cent, but because he's the father, he has rights. The system is unbelievable. What if he takes the baby? Then we'd really have a mess. He's only come once to visit, but if he comes again we'll watch him closely. No way he leaves the house with that child. His family didn't even know about the baby until two months after the birth. Fortunately, he seems to be out of the picture. He's a real loser."

Emily is the oldest of four children and she was not yet allowed to date when she became pregnant. According to her mother, she's a smart, levelheaded kid, but she was going through a period of rebellion, and one night she broke her curfew, staying out until three A.M.

"I just know that's the night it happened," Lois said. "She and I had a terrible fight before she left, and she did this to get even. My husband and I don't believe in abortion, and I'm grateful she didn't want to go that route. We thought adoption was the answer, but she wasn't willing to do that.

"We told her she couldn't live here and keep the baby. But she was so insistent on keeping it that she was willing to try to go it alone. Finally, my husband and I went to a Tough Love group and that helped a lot. Some of those parents have really awful things to work through with their teenagers.

"Using the Tough Love format as our support, we decided she and the baby could live here as long as she acted responsibly and assumed all care and financial costs of the baby. Now the baby is four months old and I must say Emily has taken to motherhood. She's nursing and she's so dang maternal you wouldn't believe it. The care of the baby is totally up to her. The baby is very healthy and weighed over eight pounds at birth. Emily took good care of herself while she was pregnant, and she's real proud of the baby.

"She'll be going to the alternative school this fall, and the baby will be in the school day-care center because I told Emily I wouldn't babysit during the day. I've got my own life. If she wants to do something special with her friends in the evening, if we're available we'll babysit.

"The first two months after we found out she was pregnant, I was constantly upset. I kept wondering what I did wrong. I blamed myself. I thought I'd delivered the message that you had to be an adult to have sex. I'm a full-time homemaker. My job is raising my kids, and it blew up in my face. I happened to attend a reunion during that time, and my best friend from high school told me her daughter had been hospitalized for attempting suicide. As we all began to open up about our children, we learned that many of us were having problems with our teenagers—drugs, alcohol, running away, you name it. In some ways pregnancy is the easiest of them all. Emily made a serious mistake but she's learned a lot from it. She's matured.

"Having a baby really limits Emily's options. We want her to go to college and we will pay for that, but she must continue to take care of all baby expenses not paid by Medicaid or the WIC program.[4] She also has to pay off the delivery expenses our insurance didn't cover. That came to about $1,600. She chips away at it with the money she earns babysitting.

"I hope she can marry and have more children someday. I still don't know why this happened. I thought I had taught her to say no.

Now I suspect she had been sexually active for a while, even though, like I said, we didn't let her date.

"I've talked to her since the baby's been born about using birth control to make sure she doesn't have another baby. She won't commit about anything that has to do with sex. I guess she thinks that has to be private.

"Sometimes I feel that parents of minors who get into situations like this have no rights, yet they have the responsibility to pay all the bills. Something's wrong with our medical system and our government. Kids can't get an aspirin without parental consent, yet they can have babies and abortions and get on birth control. It doesn't make sense.

"This whole situation hasn't been fun, but it's gone smoother than I would have predicted. Emily and I had to get some things worked out in the beginning, because she was insistent on doing everything her way, but we've gotten through it. I hate to see her missing all the good times teenagers should have. She still has two years of high school left and they're going to be very hard work.

"Emily is a good kid and she's strong. I think she's going to get through this okay. I'm willing to bet she'll pull it off."

Later, Emily talked to us. She became sexually active, she said, at a "young thirteen. The stupid part is my parents told me I couldn't date until I was sixteen. But I did lots of things they didn't know about. I had a stormy adolescence. Parents need to realize that even the real 'nice' girls are having sex these days. It's really true that everybody's doing it.

"Ryan told me he'd had an accident and couldn't have children, and like a fool I believed him. He's been awful. No help or support at all. He really fed me a line about that injury of his. And he actually had the nerve to say, 'How do I know it's mine?' I couldn't believe it. Then later he said, 'Well, even if you are, that still means eight months of free sex.'

"He's only seen the baby once. I haven't heard from him for a while, but I'm still scared he might try to get the baby. He said one time he wanted custody. He's the type who'd try that. He's already told me I'd be hearing from his lawyer. If he really cared about the baby, he'd be on my doorstep begging to make things right. His name's not on the birth certificate.

"I took the baby over to his house once because I wasn't sure if his parents even knew they had a grandchild. They were nice and held the baby and all, and we talked about the two sets of parents and Ryan and me getting together, but nothing's ever come of it. He said he'd call but of course he hasn't.

"I knew before I took a pregnancy test that I was pregnant, because my periods are real regular and I'd missed. A girlfriend and I bought one of those home kits at a drugstore and I used it in a gas station rest room. I didn't want to take a chance of someone in my family finding the box. It turned color immediately and that just confirmed it.

"I went right home and told my parents before I could lose my nerve. I never considered abortion but I did consider adopting out. I just couldn't do it. My parents said I couldn't live at home with the baby and I was going to have to try to find someplace to stay. Finally they said I could stay, but they gave me a long list of rules and regulations. I was so relieved that I could live at home that I was agreeable to anything. Now I'm getting along okay with my folks, better than I ever did before.

"I started going to the alternative school. There are lots of pregnant girls there or girls who have babies in the school day-care center. The girls are different from me, so it's hard, but I've tried to make the best of it. I wish I could go back to my old high school, but I need that day-care center. There are pregnant girls there in all the grades, from seventh through twelfth, and there's a long waiting list to get babies into the day-care center.

"I see so many problems at the center. One girl's four-year-old has rotting teeth. One girl has a three-year-old, she's had three abortions, and she's pregnant again and going to have the baby because she thinks that's the only way she can hang on to her boyfriend. There are girls who go out every night and their mothers keep their babies, and there's one girl whose boyfriend beats her up but she still leaves her baby with him so she can go out.

"One good thing about that school is that I met guys who treated me with respect because of my decision to keep the baby. They knew that was harder than having an abortion. That gives me some hope that maybe there will be a guy out there for me.

"The birth was easy and my baby is real healthy. I didn't want to get pregnant, but I know I did the right thing for me. It's going to take me a long time to get my education now, but I'm not going to be stopped."

We're willing to bet she won't be. Emily has smart parents who are requiring her to take responsibility for her child. They are doing everything the social workers at the LIGHThouse said must happen if a girl and her baby are going to do well.

But they are the exception.

A few weeks before Alex's friend Susan was due, we visited with her and with her mother, Ellen, again. Susan was excited at the baby's imminent arrival. But her excitement seemed edged with frustration and discontent, perhaps because her mother seemed to be in control of everything that was happening, almost as if she were the one expecting the baby.

Ellen was still trying to figure out her own life and was wondering about taking a job in another city, "but I wouldn't be able to leave the baby," she said tenderly.

Which made us wonder: Whose baby will this baby be? That

wasn't an issue in Emily's household. Emily *knows* she's the mother. Emily *knows* the baby is her responsibility. Will Susan?

Best estimates are that 1.2 million teenage girls get pregnant every year in this country. A teenage girl has a one-in-ten chance of being pregnant in any year, and one in four will have been pregnant before leaving her teens behind. Of those 1.2 million pregnancies, about half terminate in abortion or miscarriage and half result in live births. Very little is known about those fathers in terms of their involvement with their children or their support of them. Most teenage boys who will admit to being sexually active say they use condoms—but most teenage boys also say they are sexually active even if they aren't. Few boys are being taught sexually responsible behavior, but even if they are, like Sonya's son Jason, they may link up with a girl whose agenda is parenthood and end up with their futures severely compromised.

When a pregnancy occurs, the parents of both the girl and the boy should consult an attorney in their state of residence who practices family law. Laws vary considerably from state to state on such issues as the father's name on the birth certificate, parental rights, custody, visitation, child support, and adoption. Working out agreements on these issues before the birth can save both families heartache, disappointment, frustration, and considerable expense later.

Statistically, one in four teenage girls who gets pregnant will get pregnant again, usually within a year, whether she's miscarried, aborted, adopted out, or kept the baby. Almost always the father is a different guy, and just like the first time, she thinks he'll stick around—but he rarely does. For the other girls, the trauma of becoming pregnant is enough to make them utilize birth control or become sexually inactive.

Girls who have strong life and career goals—reasons for *not* becoming pregnant—are the most likely to opt for abortion or adopting out if they do become pregnant. They place *their* goals above raising a baby.

"Many girls get pregnant because they want someone to love or because they want their parents' attention," commented Dawn Dineen, a teacher and counselor at an alternative high school in our area where fifty-six students were either pregnant or had babies at the time we visited with her.

"I vividly remember a girl who was poor and alone with a baby who cried all the time. She was so stressed out she was afraid she would hurt the baby.

"Our older students all say they had no idea how hard it would be to care for their babies. They *all* believed their boyfriends would stay with them. Lots of boys leave when they first find out. Others make it through delivery but are gone two months later. About 85 to 90 percent of the girls say that if they knew what was in store for them, they would have aborted or adopted out.

"Most of them have poor relationships with their parents and have had little or no sex education. You can talk until you're blue in the face and they won't use protection. They think pregnancy won't happen to them."

"I agree," said Kathi Risenhoover, a counselor at the same school. "You can't make generalizations, but I also think many, if not most, of these girls consciously or subconsciously hope they will get pregnant. In some cases a pregnancy can stabilize a girl who has no goals and no close attachments.

"I also agree that many of them are looking for parental attention. Having sex has nothing to do with their parents—they aren't thinking about Mom and Dad at that moment—but getting pregnant definitely makes their parents take notice. Even if a girl has been breaking curfew, staying out late, acting out, or being sexually active, her parents may think it's just teenage rebellion and ignore it.

"Usually the parents have not discussed birth control or sex with them. When girls get pregnant, their friends tend to glamorize it, having showers for them and offering to babysit. The pregnant girl is the center of attention for a while and revels in it. Sometimes these girls become good parents, provided they have enough support around them. They have to be willing to give up a normal teen life. It's difficult for anyone to keep up with school, work, and a baby. They can't stay out late and then wake up early to a hungry baby and feel good. Sooner or later resentment crops up.

"It's also my observation that the boyfriend typically stays around for about two months after the birth and then splits. 'Let's break up for a while' is a typical statement. 'Don't worry, I'll help with the expenses. I'll buy the formula.' And then he does it for one month.

"It's very difficult for these young mothers once they finish high school and must leave all the support we give them here. If they can go to college, they may have a bright future. But most of them get bogged down in menial jobs and hard relationships. Some of them are never able to become independent of their own parents. The parents who force their daughters to assume responsibility for their children are doing them a favor. These girls are the ones most likely to become independent and take control of their lives."

Teenage girls fifteen and younger are at greatest risk in becoming parents. The younger the girl when she becomes sexually active, the greater the likelihood that she will not use birth control and that over time she will have multiple partners. If she becomes pregnant, because she may lack financial resources and physical and emotional maturity, she is at greatest risk for complications such as ectopic pregnancies, prolonged labor, premature and low-birth-weight babies, and STDs.

Children of teenage parents are at greater risk for emotional problems, lower achievement than their peers, poverty, and becoming teenage parents themselves.

According to the Family Research Council, located in Washington, D.C., 65 percent of the children born in the United States in 1992 were born out of wedlock. We also have the highest rate of teenage pregnancy in the world. Taxpayers are picking up a tab of $21.6 billion annually in aid to families of teen mothers. For the babies born to teenagers in 1989 alone, American taxpayers will kick in $6 billion over the next twenty years. In a *Wall Street Journal* article citing the dramatic rise of children living in poverty in this country, Gary Bauer, president of the Council, stated that the Children's Defense Fund "attributes the increases in poverty to structural changes in the economy, but most of the growth is due to out-of-wedlock births. No matter what the government does, if a 15-year-old has a baby, that is another impoverished household."[1]

As to what can be done to lower the rate of teenage pregnancy, the camps are divided. Conservatives push teaching abstinence. Liberals push sex education. While we all give lip service to the former, most of us feel it just won't work in today's climate of sexual permissiveness.

Still, a program called Sex Respect is now being taught in over 1,800 schools around the country, funded by monies appropriated by Congress a decade ago to teach abstinence education. In a series of ten lessons, the course teaches all the negatives of premarital sex and stresses saying no to sex. It does not discuss contraceptives or such controversial topics as homosexuality. The course has raised an army of protest from parents and educators who object to its sex stereotyping, which includes portraying teenage boys as sex predators who "aggressively seek sexual release with whatever partner they can persuade or force to accommodate them."[2]

It is our opinion that our society can work actively to help teenagers delay becoming sexually active, but at the same time, we'd better be realistic enough to teach them to use contraceptives and to make those contraceptives readily available. This will be a challenge: Only one in four sexually active teenagers between the ages of fifteen and nineteen currently uses contraception.

Along with contraception, teenagers must be taught decision-making skills. They must clearly understand actions and consequences and how to be sexually responsible. Schools, community agencies, and parents should ideally work together to educate young people, beginning in the lower elementary grades and continuing through twelfth grade. A number of exemplary programs are in place around the country. They are time-, labor-, and cost-intensive, but they do have success in lowering incidences of pregnancy (see Appendix C for resources).

Girls who opt to keep their babies need ongoing support from their families, the schools, and the community if they are to keep from quickly getting pregnant again and if they are to become financially and emotionally independent.

In the book *Adolescents at Risk*, author Joy G. Dryfoos compiled points of agreement from experts on teen-pregnancy prevention that include early intervention; a "package" of services for young people, male as well as female, that includes "both capacity-building and life-option components" and involves "provider agencies, schools, decision-makers, media, parents, and youth"; public commitment to pregnancy prevention; birth-control services and counseling; follow-up with contraceptive users; access to pregnancy testing, counseling, and abortion services; parental involvement, if possible; crisis intervention, including a twenty-four-hour hotline and referral agencies; and an array of comprehensive services, including alternative schools, preparation for employment, job placement, and case management. [3]

While we agree that such an inclusive program, taught by caring, highly trained professionals, might significantly impact our teenage population, it will take time and a supportive government and taxpayers to implement it.

In the meantime, parents *must* assume a critical role in their children's sex education and pregnancy prevention. Threats won't do it. Becoming the sex police, as we did, won't prevent teen sex.

We believe education is the only answer. We must give our children straight facts without guilt and moral judgment. We must give them all the information they need to prevent pregnancy, in frank, specific terms. We can say to them, "I wish you would wait. I feel strongly that sex should be part of a stable, committed relationship when you are older. I don't approve of your behavior. But I am giving you the information you need in the event you decide to be sexually active. Further, I want you to know you can always come to me with any concern and I will answer you as honestly as I can."

We see no realistic alternative in the wake of our nation's teen-pregnancy crisis. We believe that whether to abort, adopt out, or keep the child is rightfully the teenager's decision. We, as parents, are here for support and guidance. And they, not we, must bear the responsibility for the outcome, regardless of which very difficult path they choose.

CHAPTER 8

SEX IN A SEXUALLY UNSAFE WORLD

Both Alex and Marissa would be home in a couple of weeks, and we were getting anxious to see them. Well, we were and we weren't. We had some specific things to discuss when they returned. The sexuality education they had received from us was lacking in so many areas. So were our communication skills. We needed to make up for lost time, set some things right, and start afresh. It was both exciting and scary.

But before that happened, we felt there was one area we didn't know enough about, and that was sexually transmitted diseases, including AIDS.

Parents' hearts stop beating when the topic of AIDS comes up. We all fear for our children and grandchildren. We know about Magic Johnson and that the only truly safe sex is no sex. And we're scared to death for this next generation.

When we were teenagers and young adults, we didn't have to worry about AIDS or other STDs. Anything we were likely to get could be cured by penicillin. Our guru was Alfred E. Neuman with that crazy smile telling us, "What, me worry?" Today the best hope for our sexually active children is to convince them to use latex condoms and nonoxynol-9 spermicide, and even then, we're only making sex somewhat safer.

When you see the surveys revealing that only one in four teenagers uses any type of birth control, that one in four engages in anal sex, and that the HIV infection rate is rising rapidly in the thirteen-to-twenty-year-old age group, making sex safer looks like an uphill battle.

The information certainly is out there. AIDS came to public attention in 1981, when the first cases were noted in gay men in urban areas. Today an estimated 12 million people worldwide are infected, including a million children. Almost half of the victims are in Africa, where AIDS has depopulated whole villages of their sexually active adults. Experts estimate that up to 110 million adults and 10 million children will be infected with the virus by the year 2000. So far there is no vaccination against AIDS, and no cure for it.

In this country, over a million Americans have AIDS. In 1989 it was estimated that one in every 250 thirteen-to-twenty-year-olds carried the virus. In 1990 and part of 1991, that figure rose to one in 90, and it is expected to continue to rise.[1]

AIDS is caused by HIV (human immunodeficiency virus), which attacks the cells in the immune system, affecting the body's ability to fight off infection. You can be HIV-positive for years, passing it to other people the whole time, and never be sick or even know you have it unless you get tested.

Eventually the HIV infection becomes AIDS (acquired immunodeficiency syndrome), when your immune system can no longer protect you from such illnesses as pneumonia, certain cancers, tuberculosis, and various infections. AIDS kills when the body becomes too weak to fight off these illnesses.

AIDS is spread through vaginal, anal, or oral sex; through transfusions of infected blood; through the sharing of infected needles used to inject drugs; and from infected mothers to infants during birth.

HIV is passed more readily to women from men, than to men from women. In fact, studies show that infected men are twice as likely to pass it to women as women are to pass it on to men.

Other sexually transmitted diseases are also putting our young people at risk. Syphilis and gonorrhea are increasing. So are ectopic pregnancies and infertility from STDs. Herpes and the virus that causes genital warts can't be cured. Gonorrhea and chlamydia can cause sterility and also harm newborns.

The most common STDs, infecting 2.5 to 3 million new American teenagers each year, include:

Chlamydia: Painful urination, pelvic pain, vaginal or penile discharge, and/or genital itching can all signal chlamydia in males or females. It is the most common STD and can lead to sterility in women. It is silent in the early stages, when it is doing its damage. Caught in time, it can be treated.

Genital herpes: There's no cure for herpes simplex virus, and 500,000 Americans are newly diagnosed with it every year. It causes cold sore–like lesions in the genital area, and outbreaks come and go. Women with active lesions can infect babies during birth, causing brain damage or death. It can only be passed between partners when lesions are active.

Genital warts: Genital warts, caused by certain types of the human papilloma virus (HPV), also have no cure, although doctors can remove them. However, HPV may remain in the body after the warts are removed, and recurrence is common. Self-diagnosis is difficult because the warts may appear inside the cervix or vagina in women. Men get these small bumps, too, usually near the rectum, and there may be a link between the warts and the development of cancers of the penis, vulva, and cervix. An estimated one million Americans contract the warts annually.

Gonorrhea: This STD affects many more blacks than whites and is often present at the same time as chlamydia. In women the infection can affect the fallopian tubes and cause infertility or tubal pregnancy. It can also affect a child's eyes at birth if the mother is infected. Typical symptoms are genital burning, itching, discharge, painful urination, breakthrough bleeding between periods, abdominal pain, or vomiting. Left untreated, it can lead to blindness, heart or brain problems, arthritis, skin sores, and even death.

Hepatitis B: A vaccine is available against this virus that can lead to cirrhosis or liver cancer, but few people get it. While there is no cure, most people do recover on their own from the flulike illness and jaundice, but they still may have liver problems down the line. Hepatitis B isn't always classified as an STD because sex is only one of the ways it's spread. It infects about 300,000 Americans every year and causes 5,000 deaths.

PID: Pelvic inflammatory disease can be caused by gonorrhea or chlamydia. An infection in the cervix and fallopian tubes, it can scar the tubes and prevent or complicate pregnancy. Experts estimate that over 400,000 women seek treatment every year.

Syphilis: Centuries old, syphilis has flared anew in the last decade and now affects over 100,000 Americans every year. It causes genital lesions and without treatment leads to fever, aches, rash, and other problems. In its late stages it can affect the major organs of the body. Pregnant women can also pass it to their unborn children. While the damage from syphilis to the body cannot be undone, antibiotics can prevent it from advancing.

Regarding birth control, teenagers have a range of options apart from the condom—which is absolutely necessary *in addition* to another form of birth control in order to prevent STDs. Far too many teens rely on the rhythm method (charting "safe" days) or withdrawal before ejaculation. Both have high failure rates. The next most popular method is the pill, but it does require an examination, a prescription, and the diligence to take the pill daily. It works through use of a synthetic hormone to inhibit development of eggs.

Some teenage girls are agreeing to the Norplant implant. It gives them five years of protection and, like the pill, is very effective. It's costly up front—$400 to $700—but is no more costly in the long run than pill prescriptions. Implanted in the underside of the arm, it looks like small matchsticks and works via synthetic progestin to suppress ovulation, fertilization, and implantation.

Less popular with teenage girls are diaphragms, the cervical cap, the IUD, and the sponge, all of which block sperm or inhibit fertilization and implantation. Spermicides—which come in cream, jelly, foam, and suppository forms—also kill or immobilize sperm, and they are readily available at drugstores. The drawback teens complain about is that they "break the mood." All teenagers, however, should be using a spermicide with nonoxynol-9, whether they use condoms or another form of birth control, because it has been shown to be effective in killing the AIDS virus.

A recent development, not yet widely available, is the female condom that the female inserts into the vagina before having sex. It's effective protection against pregnancy and STDs but may be perceived by teens as cumbersome and unattractive (another "mood breaker"). If a male refuses to wear a condom, however, and the female wants to have sex with him, this is a safe alternative.

In the works are more effective morning-after pills, a contraceptive pill for men, and a home urine test that instantly measures the hormone level in women that signals ovulation and thus indicates whether contraception is necessary.

Ideally, sexually active young people should be checked twice a year for STDs, and sexually active girls should have a yearly pelvic exam and Pap smear. Since most teenagers won't even go to the doctor for regular medical checkups, prevention is the best chance of keeping these problems under control.

Too many parents think that once a child reaches the teen years, regular checkups are no longer necessary. Teens don't get colds and earaches as frequently as younger children, nor do they need a series of immunizations.

Teens *do*, however, need to have a doctor following their growth, weight, physical development, blood pressure, and cholesterol levels. Doctors will also screen for problems like headaches, stomachaches, scoliosis (curvature of the spine), and vision changes.

They will also look at such psychosocial issues as depression, eating disorders, and substance abuse. Family doctors are also ready to discuss sexual activity and contraception, but it's a rare teenager who feels comfortable enough with the family doctor to do this, either out of embarrassment or from fear that the doctor will inform the family. Examinations are also hard for teenagers, many of whom are very private about their bodies.

In a society with a generation of young people at risk medically, the clinics may be our best hope. Teenagers know that they will receive free or very low-cost care, that they won't be lectured, that nobody will recognize them, and that their parents won't be informed of their visits. When such clinics are located near schools or colleges and dispense free condoms and other forms of birth control, huge numbers of young people use them.

But parents tend to feel uncomfortable about them. We did. We had a bias against what we thought of as storefront medicine. A friend referred to them as "docs in a box." We didn't believe anybody could get quality care in a place where different medical personnel did every examination and medical facilities were fairly simple.

That bias disappeared when we actually went to a county health-care clinic popular with teenagers and talked to some of the staff.

Three nurse practitioners, all licensed to perform medical exams, said they were delighted to meet two concerned parents and gave us a generous slice of their clinic time to visit with us. These three women—Marianne, Barbara, and Micki—represent three generations. All three spoke in quiet, gentle, concerned voices.

"Most of the teenagers we see are girls, and they are here without their parents' knowledge," commented Barbara. "Some parents object to us because they think we're too liberal. Others are afraid, as you said you are, that their child won't get professional enough care. But the way we see it is that we give excellent care and teens will come to us when they won't go to their family doctor for fear of disclosure or because of embarrassment. They will also come to us because they know their parents won't find out."

"The exception is if a teen needs some special tests or needs to see a specialist," Marianne added. "Occasionally we do have to get parents involved, and that often poses a problem.

"We have to take our cues from the teen. She is the best judge of how to involve the parents. Sometimes it just takes a phone call from one of us. Most teenagers are very afraid of how their parents will respond. It's true that some parents just don't care—or can't be found. But most are willing to get involved."

"Sometimes we have to involve them because a teen needs some expensive treatment that we must charge for," Micki said, "and many parents have insurance. Otherwise the girl has to pay for it herself.

Tests can run to hundreds of dollars, and that's tough to pay off when you have a part-time minimum-wage job."

"We try to get the kids to talk to their parents, but we aren't always successful. Ideally, parents would come with their teens for medical care. In reality, not all parents are approachable when it comes to sex, which is why it's important that our services be confidential, even though that angers many parents," Barbara added. "It's a dilemma. If we didn't provide these services on a confidential basis, we wouldn't see these kids at all. We tell the ones who come here that they are the responsible ones. We always try to compliment them. Our biggest medical problem as a society is the ones who won't come even to us—the girls who go to an emergency room ready to deliver their babies when they've never seen a physician."

"Our services are fairly comprehensive. We do complete physicals, we do Pap smears, we check for STDs, we dispense birth control, and if it's requested, we do an HIV screening," Micki explained. "We're seeing more STDs, but we're also screening more teenagers than ever. We spend forty-five minutes to an hour with each patient. If a girl needs to make an appointment with one of our physicians, she can request a female physician."

"When a girl makes an appointment, we encourage her to bring her friends along. If they come, it's not unusual for them to end up making appointments for themselves," Marianne said. "Most of these girls want birth control. Typically they've been sexually active for six months to a year without using anything and they're getting worried.

"In spite of being students, most of them know very little about their anatomy, so we educate them quite a bit. The younger girls— the twelve- and thirteen-year-olds we see are more likely to be taking chances with unprotected sex. The younger girls who have babies are also more likely to not use protection afterward—which puts them at risk for having another baby right away."

"There are days when I just have to go into the office and let out my feelings after trying to deal with some of these kids," said Barbara in frustration. "Sometimes you can predict the ones who are headed for trouble—the ones you send away from a contraceptive visit with pills in hand and they still come back pregnant a few months later."

Marianne also expressed frustration. "When you talk to these kids about sex education, usually you learn that they've either had none or they've had a five-minute talk about the birds and the bees. Most of them get more information from television than they do from their parents. None of them are being taught about risks and consequences. Kids these days just don't learn decision-making skills. And in typical teenage fashion, they never think anything will happen to them."

"You mentioned the media, and I think it's partly to blame for what's going on," Micki said thoughtfully. "TV is giving teenagers the message that they can jump in and out of bed with anyone they want to and there's never any problem. These kids believe that sex is just a recreational activity like anything else. Their parents aren't home much—in fact, finding a place to have sex is no problem at all."

"I feel sorry for teenagers because they have so many really serious issues to face. When I was a teenager," Barbara said, "my own home was the last place I would have had sex, in part because my mother was always there. And I wouldn't have known where to get alcohol. The only place it was served in my town was the bar, and I would certainly have never gone in there. But today, beer is served at Pizza Hut. Ads for it are all over TV. Drug pushers are in the school hallways. Sex has always led to pregnancy, but now one encounter can be fatal.

"And so many of these girls are being pressured to have sex. We see young women coming in for HIV or STD testing and they'll tell us, 'I was with this guy and he made me have sex with him.' It's happening a lot. Boys play at love to get sex and girls play at sex to get love. I've heard that for years and I believe it."

"So often it's when a girl comes in for a pregnancy test that we have our first opportunity to talk to her about birth control," said Marianne. "Boys rarely come in for birth control. We'll dispense condoms if they go through a clinic visit. But usually the only time we see them is if they need to be tested for an STD or HIV. A few boyfriends come along with pregnant girlfriends, but they often disappear later on.

"Fortunately the child-support laws are finally starting to get some teeth in them and these young fathers are having to take some responsibility."

"But," added Micki, "the problem is, so many of the girls—this is true for women, too—can't name the father. They'll ask for the exact date we think they got pregnant, and even then they don't always know.

"I worry a lot about the self-esteem of these girls. They seem to think having sex with a boy is the only way to have a boyfriend. They also put up with such lousy treatment because they're so desperate for a guy's attention. They'll make comments like 'I just do it because he likes it.' They don't even know about orgasm or female pleasure. Everything is for the guy."

"And they move from partner to partner so fast," added Marianne. "It's serial monogamy—six weeks with this guy, four with the next, and sex with all of them. Yet they rarely feel comfortable discussing birth control with any of them because they don't know them well enough."

"Too many of them never see positive, permanent relationships," Barbara said. "They don't know that two people can live happily together for many years in a sexually exclusive relationship because it isn't modeled for them by their parents *or* the media.

"As upsetting as it is to the parents of a sixteen-year-old girl who comes to us and gets herself on birth control," Micki said, "we hope they realize that she's being responsible. She values herself enough to protect herself, and she also thinks enough of her partner—and of her parents—to do that. These kids are often much more realistic about all this than their parents are."

Marianne brought our session to a close. "So many adults still have their head in the sand," she said. "A friend of mine who's a public librarian here in the county told me the other day that they had to take a book on the body written for young people off the shelf because a parent saw the word 'masturbation' in it and got fifty other parents to sign a petition requesting its removal. Instead of parents protecting their children, these days it's often the other way around."

Our session with these wise women changed our ideas about clinics. Before, we had worried about the possibility of one of our daughters' going to one, but now we could see the wisdom of such a decision. As a rule, the care and treatment are high-quality, medical details are attended to, and problems are handled with respect, concern, and confidentiality. Few of us can ask more of the medical profession.

Joan Mansfield, a pediatrician who is on the Harvard Medical School faculty and whose practice is devoted to adolescent gynecology at Boston Children's Hospital, told us that when it comes to their children's sex lives, parents should realize that even sons and daughters they completely trust may lie to them.

"It's been my experience that parents sometimes *think* they have open and honest communication with their teens and find out later they've lied about something they've been doing for years.

"Also," she said, "parents have a hard time accepting that teens are making choices that often involve risky behaviors. If you want to be there to help them, you've got to be flexible about some of this. We know, for example, that four in ten girls get pregnant sometime in their teen years.

"If parents make ultimatums like, 'If you ever get pregnant, I'll kick you out,' then you've got trouble, because the kids are so worried about parental reaction that they won't seek medical attention when they need it."

Basing her judgment on her years in practice, she sees the best resolution of parent-teen problems over sex when parents have kept channels of communication open.

"Don't isolate yourself from your teenagers," she suggested. "They need you and they don't want to disappoint you. They make the wisest choices they can, based on their individual experience. I think it's a mistake for parents to step in and make a decision about what to do when a daughter becomes pregnant. It may not be the best choice for her, and it can create later risks for repeat pregnancy, depression, and suicide. Parents and very young teens should make the decision together.

"I don't think parents should wait for their children to question them about sex. Use the opportunities provided by the media to bring up the subject. Ask your child's opinion and listen to and acknowledge the answer, then add your thoughts. Explain why you believe the way you do and be clear about your values, while leaving room for your child to differ.

"I think adolescence is a very exciting time of life. It's full of risks, but also full of possibilities, and teens can and do learn from their mistakes. Give them your trust and give them the benefit of the doubt."

That was something we knew we hadn't done with either of our daughters. We *said* we trusted them, yet we hovered above them, trying to double-check on what they were doing and with whom. Could we give them the benefit of the doubt?

Yes, we agreed, *provided* we knew we'd given them all the information they needed to protect themselves in a sexually unsafe world and to make wise choices—not the choices that were best for us but the choices that were best for them.

A tall order for the two of us. A tall order for any loving parent. But knowing you've done all you can do is clearly the only way to get a good night's sleep and to let them get one, too.

Changes were going to take place in our household.

CHAPTER 9

FULL CIRCLE

We were feeling like battle-weary veterans. Ever since our daughters had gone away, we'd submerged ourselves in issues pertaining to teens and sex. We knew much more, we were much more comfortable with the topic, and we had a pretty good idea of what we had to do and say when they got home.

We had only ten days until they returned when a last unique opportunity came our way. We ran into an old friend who works in the counseling center at a nearby college and told her of our quest for understanding about teenage sexuality and how parents and teens can peacefully coexist on this issue.

She said she would be happy to pull together a few college students who were helping with the summer orientation programs for incoming freshmen and parents if we would like to visit with some young people in their early twenties.

We jumped at the chance. The young people were still close enough in age to the issues not to have forgotten them. At the same time, they were in touch with seventeen- and eighteen-year-olds and their families—a reminder of what they had been like at that age.

We thought they could lend insight into what parents of teenagers may face in the next few years.

So on a sweltering late-July day we sat down with six delightful young people, ages twenty to twenty-three, to discuss issues for parents regarding teens and sex. As our friend had assured us, they were friendly and willing to talk and had a lot to say. Just listen:

Cindi, a twenty-year-old French major who aspires to work for the United Nations, spoke first.

"The sex education I got in school was such a joke," she said, rolling her eyes. "The word 'condom' might have been mentioned twice. The teacher didn't want to discuss the tough issues, and the parents didn't want him to. Anything I knew I learned from friends."

"My mother taught me," said Nichole, a secondary education major. "She's a nurse and knows what's going on. She's not afraid to talk about it. She's very straightforward. I know I could tell her anything and she would be there for me, even if she disapproved. My father, on the other hand, doesn't know *anything* about my private life, and he doesn't want to. It's all left up to my mom."

"My mom made it clear to me that she doesn't approve of sex outside of marriage, but what I appreciate in looking back is that she taught me to think about consequences," Kyla said. "I want to be a pediatrician and I plan to do the same thing with my teenage patients. 'If you practice this and this behavior, then here's what could happen.' That kind of stuff. I started having sex my senior year of high school, but I was ready. I prepared myself because that's what I'd been taught to do."

"You had such with-it parents," said Greg, shaking his head in disbelief. "I come from a fundamentalist Christian home in a little town out in western Kansas, and I swear everybody in town was sexually repressed. We weren't told anything. Not in school, in church, or at home. Maybe it's because I was so curious all the time that I'm a journalism major. My sex education consisted of one sentence my mother said to me when I was about sixteen and going out on a date. She said, 'Keep your pants on and your feet on the floor.' And that was *it*."

"I have a friend like that and she's a mess," Kyla said. "Her family is strict Mormon. She was told a little bit about her period and then it was made very clear that you are a virgin until your wedding night. She's been sexually active all through college, and the guilt just eats her up. If her parents found out they would probably disown her. I said that just can't be true, but she said it absolutely is.

"What I don't understand is all the risks she takes. She's already had one abortion and just recently she had an AIDS test because for a while she dated this scuzzy senior who's a needle user and she got scared. If somebody would have talked to her way back, maybe she would be okay."

"Most students have lives that are secret from their parents," offered Lance, a twenty-year-old theater major from Wisconsin. "Once you move out, they can't see you and know what you're up to. They have no idea how many students sleep around and with how many people. In orientation sessions we tell parents that 70 percent of incoming freshmen are sexually active. Parents don't believe it. What we *don't* tell them is that by the end of their freshman year, about 95 percent of college students are sexually active. That doesn't mean all the time, but at least occasionally."

"Or maybe 99 percent," added Rob, a business major from the West Coast. "It seems like it's everybody at one time or another. It's not a big deal in college like it was in high school. We think of ourselves as adults and this is something adults do."

"We probably do it more than the regular adult population," Nichole said, laughing. "It's like everyone's been told for so long not to do it, that when you get there, you jump right in."

"Maybe 99 percent of the guys do it, but a lot of women in

my dorm don't even have boyfriends," commented Cindi. "So I think that's an exaggeration. Whether it is or isn't, who cares? That's what changes in college. In high school, everybody cares."

"Parents still care," Nichole said. "I went camping recently with my boyfriend. My mother knows we sleep together and we're probably going to share an apartment together next year. But my dad got real upset when he heard about the camping. My mother told him that nothing was going to happen there that wouldn't go on anyway, but he just wouldn't accept that. He's totally oblivious to that part of my life."

"He doesn't want to know," Kyla said. "At one level he does, but you're his little girl still, and he doesn't want to be reminded that you have sex. Fathers view daughters very differently than mothers do. Mothers are realistic. They know what's going on."

Greg disagreed. "*Some* mothers do. Mine didn't. I'm angry that neither of my parents acknowledge my puberty. Nothing was ever said to me. My friends and I all grew up in these families where nobody talked to us. Now we all have hangups about things like homosexuality and violence and sex. I swear if my sister had gotten pregnant my parents would have shipped her off somewhere to have the baby, put the baby up for adoption, and then brought her home and locked her up in a dark room the rest of her life to punish her."

"The real point about college students and sex is that many of us are doing it and we enjoy it and we're putting our lives in danger and we still can't talk about it. That makes it extremely important," Lance said. "One in five college students has an STD, one in nine college women will have an unplanned pregnancy. They have abortions all the time. Date rape happens way too much. We estimate that one in eight women are raped while they're at college, and they almost always know the guy. When we ask parents in the orientation classes how many of them have talked to their kids about sex, they all raise their hands. Every one of them. But when we ask a group of seventy-five incoming freshmen the same thing, four or five raise their hands, ten tops. Teenagers want *real* information, not the birds and the bees."

"We're a sick country," Rob said. "It doesn't make any sense that people get so upset about people in the movies or on television making love, but they'll pay big bucks to watch two men beating the hell out of each other in the boxing ring. We glorify the violence, but we freak out at the natural instinct to have sex."

"I think males are more aggressive now than they were when we were in high school," Greg said. "Look at the talk shows and all the sick stuff they bring to us every day. The soaps are pure sex. We are completely overwhelmed with all these sexual images, especially ones that drive adolescent males completely wild.

"I didn't have the experience of MTV pumping these incredible willing women into my mind every day. Bad enough when it started in high school. If it had started when I was twelve or thirteen, I think it would have really changed my ideas of what I thought was mine for the taking or what I could look forward to. I think that's why date rape is up. That and all the alcohol we all drink here."

"Between the ads and the shows, TV *is* sex," Rob said. "Even the Gulf War, when it was going on. I think it was a very sexual experience for a lot of adolescent guys and college-age men. I'd watch it on TV with my fraternity brothers. So many got off on the power. It was a totally sexual experience for them. They were practically orgasmic when they'd watch these missiles go through the doors and explode. It is absolutely amazing how sexual that imagery is. It wasn't much different from watching Madonna on MTV."

"I plan to be a high school history teacher, so I go into the schools to observe. I can't believe how much things have changed in a few short years," said Nichole, who's twenty-one. "The language in the hallways and the sex stuff, the kissing and body touching you see if teachers aren't looking."

"But a few important things haven't changed at all," commented Lance. "For one of my theater classes I helped out with a high school play. Some of the kids were telling me about the sex-education unit in their health class. They were making jokes about it, but I think they were as insulted as I was when I took it in high school, because you don't really get told anything. Kids need to know about AIDS and STDs but it's hardly touched on. You just get biology. When I took it, every one of us knew about sexual intercourse and a lot of us were doing it, but the teacher never once mentioned it. It's the same today. With all the problems out there, the kids need information and the schools need to do something."

"A coach taught my class. I think he must have been assigned to do it, because he treated the whole thing like a joke," Cindi said. "My friends and I thought it was crap. Our attitude was to just tune out adults. Why waste your time on them, because they're going to play games with you."

"My family was a lot like Greg's," Rob said. "I wasn't told much of anything because my parents were just so scared of it. And there was nothing at school. I did some pretty stupid things when I got to college. I think I'm a sensitive guy now, but I was really a jerk with a couple of girls. I fought with my penis all the time. There's just a lot of mythology that goes with growing up male in this country. Kids need to know about birth control by the time they start junior high, because that's when a lot of them start to have sex."

"Since I was raised with all this fire-and-brimstone religion, I was taught that I'd go to hell if I sinned, and carnal knowledge and all that was definitely a sin," Greg added. "Even now I struggle with those images when I'm with a woman. It makes me angry. The interesting thing was, the girls I went to church with were the loosest of all when it came to morals. Maybe it's the preacher's-daughter syndrome. Some of the stories about those girls were just amazing. And probably not true."

"My parents never gave me the Big Talk," Lance said, "but my mom had this way of making sure I got the information anyway. I had access to books and pamphlets and stuff. My parents had this book on sex in their nightstand, and I knew where every juicy passage was. Now I know I was played like a deck of cards. My mom knew I was reading all those things, and she knew that even though I found all the good parts, I was reading the other stuff too."

"You can see it with the incoming freshmen," Kyla said. "The ones whose parents are giving them the hardest time and are trying to make all decisions for them will be the wildest when they get here. It never fails. You can see it in the eyes of the girls who look at their mothers and are silently calling them bitches. They go nuts when they get away from their parents, because they've never been allowed to take responsibility for themselves. By the time you're ready to go to college, parents have got to accept that you have your own mind and your own beliefs and you'll do what you want."

"It's true," Nichole agreed. "When you move away from home to start college, your relationship with your parents should change. They need to accept you on a more equal basis and be friends with you. By the time you're eighteen you begin to understand that your parent is actually a person and has had a life apart from just being your parent. When I was eighteen my mother told me she had gotten pregnant at my age and had an abortion and it was very hard for her. After that she had been real depressed and started using alcohol and diet pills. She told me because she didn't want that to happen to me. But what it also did was make her real to me. I had a whole new understanding of my mother after that."

"I can't imagine my parents at sixteen or eighteen," Greg said. "They always told me I could come to them with anything, but I knew very well I couldn't go to them with squat. Alcohol was a very big part of my life while I was in high school, and I needed to talk to an adult about it, but I knew I couldn't let them be disappointed in me, so even though I might come home smelling of beer or weaving a little bit, I stayed far enough away from them so they wouldn't notice. And they didn't. They never proved to me that I could trust them with anything important in my life."

"I can talk to my parents about anything *except* sex," Cindi said. "My mother claims she never saw a naked man until her wedding night, and somehow I just don't buy it. It sounds so unrealistic to me. When it comes to sex, the only message I get is, Wait until you're married. It's like, get married and suddenly you'll know everything you need to know. I doubt that it works that way."

"I can't imagine my parents as teenagers," Rob said. "They were married at nineteen and twenty and that's already three years ago for me. It's scary. I see my mother as pretty pure. I can't imagine she ever had a boyfriend other than my father. I don't have a concept of Mom and Dad as sexual. Maybe if parents could convince us early that they actually had a life, we wouldn't reject them later on. They try to present this image as perfect and all-knowing, and then something will happen and they'll say, 'I know just how you feel,' and it doesn't work unless you've had that all along."

"By the time we get to college, our parents shouldn't try to tell us what to do anymore," Lance said. "If they could think back to when they were our age, maybe it would help. I realized my mom was actually a person about the time I turned twenty, because she stopped acting like a parent and started acting like a friend. But we fought the whole time I was in high school."

"We know what values our parents want us to have," Kyla said, "so they don't have to keep after us about that. But this is the time in our lives to try different things. It doesn't mean we abandon our parents' values. Parents need to stop saying the words, 'How could you do this to me?' and 'Why are you doing this to me?' We aren't even thinking of them!"

"Parents will never accept what we do. It's always that way between generations," Nichole said. "But they still should inform us about everything just to make sure we know it. My mom's always sending

me newspaper articles about AIDS and condoms and stuff. My boyfriend gets upset about it, but I know it's just her way of getting
information to me, and I don't mind."

"Just so she's also educating you about relationships," Kyla responded. "She knows you have sex, so she should also be sending
you the articles about understanding your partner and taking care of
the person you have sex with and learning how to talk to him. Sex
is not just a physical act."

"I think parents teach best by example," Cindi said. "They may
have trouble with the words and use articles and books, and that's
okay. What really matters is what they model for us. What is ingrained
in us is what we observed growing up."

"I agree with that," said Greg. "My parents didn't tell me anything,
and I plan to help my own kids know everything. I want them to feel
comfortable with their bodies. I want them to know that there are
many facets to a healthy, fulfilling sexual relationship. It's communication, it's getting through the role mythology, it's the act itself.
When we're teenagers, we start practicing all that. We do it on a
miniature scale. Parents are the ones who can help their kids get it
right. And then they can't do any more. They have to let go."

And that, we contend, is exactly what most parents desire very ear-
nestly to do. We want our children to have their own lives so we can
have ours.

So that this transition is successful for them and for us, both our
sons and our daughters should know some of the problems they or friends
may encounter and how to respond to them. Here are some examples:

▶ According to a survey, one in four college men and one in
    six college women think a man has a right to force his date
    to have sex with him if he's spent money on her.

▶ College women are often the target of sexual harassment by college men and/or male faculty—and men can also be harassed by women.

▶ Increasing numbers of college students leave their campuses as alcoholics, and alcohol plays a role in a majority of date rapes and unwanted pregnancies. Young men who drink and who think they've got a green light from their dates can quickly get out of control and force themselves on women who are unsuspecting and unwilling. Young women who drink may lose control as well.

Young women who go directly to jobs or to the service out of high school can encounter these same problems. The more we can do to help our teenagers respond assertively if these problems arise, the better protected they will be.

Our daughters must also know that dating and sex aren't as romantic as they might wish them to be. If we've learned anything from the Mike Tyson rape trial, it's that young women must not get themselves into situations where they may be forced to have sex. Date rape is real and frightening, and, in this day of AIDS and other STDs, dangerous.

At the same time, since the odds are that most of them will have at least occasional sexual encounters in the ensuing years, it's good to remind them that sex is almost always the most satisfying in a loving, caring relationship in which each partner looks after the other's welfare.

A while back we met a woman at a pool party who was wearing a T-shirt that showed a haggard woman, martini in hand, with copy above her reading, "Listen, honey—nobody knows how to raise teenagers. . . . You just live through it and one day they're people!" She asked if we had children. Two teenage daughters, we said, smiling at her shirt. A mock-serious expression came over her face. "Oh, you have my condolences," she said.

She reminded us of a good friend who told us several years ago that he didn't want to have children because he couldn't imagine letting another human being to do to him what he did to his parents when he was a teenager. But life goes on, and now he has two preschoolers of his own. Just recently we jokingly reminded him of his statement. He looked stricken. "I'm going to have to figure out some kind of strategy before my kids hit their teens," he said. "I just can't be on the receiving end of that garbage teens hand to their parents. Right now I try not to think about it so I can enjoy my kids while they're little."

We talked to a young woman of twenty-five who told us that she wishes she could forget eighteen months of her adolescence.

"You wouldn't believe how awful I was. I was so mean to my mother, I sneaked out, I lied, I stole, I was doing it with a bunch of different guys—oh, I was the worst!" she said, covering her face with her hands in embarrassment. "I don't know how my parents survived it. I can't even remember what they did, except they hung in there. They didn't give up on me. Eventually some sort of common sense kicked in and then I was okay."

We've heard these stories over and over again. Most young adults tell us their parents had no idea of all the things they were doing, the risks they were taking to their health and well-being. In some instances they suspect their parents knew but had made a conscious decision to let them sink or swim.

When our children leave home to take on the world, we're not going to be there when problems arise. We must trust them. If we've done our work well, they will be able to take responsibility for themselves.

We will have to let go.

CHAPTER 10

RESOLUTION

Teenagers, we now know, ask the impossible of us. They want us to be there, loving and supporting and guiding them, but at the same time they want us to stand out of the way.

They want us to talk openly and honestly to them, but they don't want us telling them anything they don't want to hear.

They are curious about sex and want us to provide them with information, but they don't want us asking them personal questions. Sex is, in fact, the topic they are most reluctant to talk about with parents.

In discussions of sex, as in every other area of their lives, they push us away, determined to be independent and to form their own identities. In spite of our desire to offer them the benefit of our experience, they want to be allowed to make their own mistakes, discounting our knowledge with a self-righteous wail of "You just don't understand."

In order to exert their independence from us, they will operate on the principle "If you say something is black I'm going to say it's white, if you say yes I'm going to say no, if you say do it this way

I'm going to do it that way, if you're a Republican then I'm a Democrat."

By going back and remembering what we were like as teenagers, we parents will recall that we did the same thing with our own parents. Just as we did, our teenagers *must* separate from us. They *must* be their own people. They *must* find an identity apart from us. When they were babies, they thought they *were* us. When they were young children, they wanted to be *like* us. Until they were eleven or twelve, they thought we were smart, and they wanted to do things with us, and they even wanted to hold hands with us.

When puberty hits, most children start to pull away. They have demanding work to do in their teen years: They must stop being us, and become themselves. Sometimes, the closer they have been to us, the harder they must fight to separate from us and the more outrageous will be the signs and behaviors of their declaration of independence.

Up to this point we have been the controlling force in their lives. Now we're expected to gradually give up our control, and this is no easy task for us if we haven't been working at it all along. We understand that if we don't do it successfully we will have created dependent adult children who will have difficulty living their own lives. Still, letting go is a struggle for us. Teenagers vary, but one thing we know for sure is that at least to some degree our teenagers *will* do what they want. If we get in the way, they will figure out how to get around us. If we force them to become secretive, they will. If we force them to lie to us to keep us happy, they will. If we keep them from doing something they want to do, they will somehow retaliate. We *cannot* win the struggle for control, so it's just a question of how smooth or rough the process of handing it over will be, and how much guilt and hostility we want to create.

Teenagers don't want us to dump it in their laps. They want it to be given over to them in an orderly fashion. They know, at least subconsciously, that they are not ready for it all at once. Also—and this surprises many parents who are in an adversarial relationship with their children—they *want* to be friends with us, or at least be friendly with us.

As much as our teenagers seem to hate us much of the time, the truth is, even as we are relinquishing our control, *they want to be accountable to us.* They want us to be part of their lives. They want to be able to trust us more than anybody else in the world. And they want us to stop them when they're about to make self-destructive mistakes. In other words, they want to look up to adults and learn from adults. Unfortunately, because there's so much about this process of human development we don't understand, we often disappoint them. Sometimes we make judgments, we punish, we even lie. We may be unwilling to see things from their point of view or incapable of doing so.

Most of us try hard. We don't want to be inflexible or unreasonable. Until they become parents themselves, they'll never know how hard it is to have to say no to them so often. Saying yes or saying and doing nothing is so much easier. But "yes" is often a panacea for the short run—it makes life pleasant for the moment. "No" is for the long run, for long-range character development. It helps our children learn to say no. We must remember that.

Child rearing is tough under any circumstances, and never more so than in this day of credit-card mentality, when kids assume from watching the Home Shopping Channel and all the sexual encounters they see on television and at the movies that you can have what you want right this moment and not have to worry about paying for it until later.

But when it comes to sex in the nineties, when it's time to pay up, the stakes can be deadly. We parents often wish we could lock our children away or convince them to remain celibate in order to protect them. But one thing that has never changed about teenagers and never will is the belief "It won't happen to me." Some kids— make that *most* kids—have to learn for themselves.

As tough as teenagers are on us, they're no easier on themselves. They are full of conflict and self-doubt. Their hormones are raging and they want to explore the feel-good feelings that go with sex. At the same time, they're very anxious about sex. They worry continuously about their physical appearance and how they are perceived by the opposite sex. If they are experimenting with sex, they worry about sexual performance and what their partners say about them to their friends.

Our generation grew up pressured to remain sexually pure. Girls with no interest in "going all the way" with a guy could comfortably say no, since that was society's expectation. But if a girl cared for a guy and *wanted* to have sex, she may have been racked with guilt about it, or incredibly frustrated if she didn't.

Today virginity weighs heavily on teens by age fifteen (and considerably earlier in some settings). Both sexes face peer pressure, encouragement from the media, and a belief that "everybody's doing it," making it difficult for them to stay outside the mainstream of sexual activity, even if they don't feel ready, or, for lots of reasons, don't want to participate. If they don't do it, they may be subject to cruel teasing, usually focused on sexual orientation ("You a queer, or what?" "She's a lesbo").

Boys are pressured to "score," to chalk up the proverbial notches on the bedpost. Girls face the dilemma of trying to walk a delicate line between being popular and being called a slut if they dare sleep with too many boys. If they begin having sex, they worry about getting caught in the act by the police, parents, or other adults. Girls worry about pregnancy. Nobody worries nearly enough about STDs.

If they haven't become sexually active, they worry about the first time: when, where, with whom. They wonder what sex feels like.

They worry that other kids think there's something wrong with them—so they frequently lie and say they've done it. Few of them are boastful of their virginity. To "save it for my wedding night" is a notion too old-fashioned to be seriously contemplated by the majority of young people today, even those taking sex-education classes emphasizing chastity.

Adolescents with sexual-orientation issues to work out may have the toughest time of all. They are struggling to accept themselves. Many of them are trying to decide whether to tell their parents. In the meantime they must keep up appearances with friends and society. They may feel they are living a lie, carrying an impossibly heavy burden. Unless they are openly gay or lesbian (and few teens are), they may be loners or date just for appearance sake. Bereft of society's sanction, they are not able to enjoy the support, the personal growth and insight, and the pleasure that can come from dating.

We parents are having struggles of our own. Just as our children must separate from us, we must also separate from them. We're struggling with letting go, with coming to terms with the fact that our children will do things counter to our beliefs and the values we have raised them with because they are themselves—unique individuals. They are *not us*.

As loving parents, we want our sons and daughters to enjoy their teen years, to go out with other kids and have a good time. We know that dating is important during these years, because this is how they learn to relate to the opposite sex and to find out what kind of person suits them best. So we are supportive and encouraging of this behavior even as it scares us to death.

The issue of teens and sex has many of us on pins and needles. If they settle in and date one person for a while, we start to get nervous. Are they having sex? If so, are they able to discuss critical issues like birth control openly and honestly? Should we try to stop them from having sex? Is it best to say nothing—or to talk talk talk? Should we try to break them up? Should we ignore it all and hope it goes away?

From our discussions with parents, we have learned that mothers are usually the ones who blame themselves when their sons and daughters get sick, fail a course, become sexually active (particularly daughters), declare their homosexuality, or do anything else viewed as a problem. "Where did I go wrong?" "How did I fail?" And the most punishing words of all—"if only." "If only I'd taken you to a doctor." "If only I'd been more strict [or "more lenient"]." "If only your father had been home more." "If only I'd understood what you were really saying to me." Fathers seem much more able to put it all in perspective, to say "That's life," or "The kid is going to do what he wants, and you can't stop him."

Many parents and teens continue to struggle with the issue of control for years to come. You see it even in adults in their sixties whose eighty-five-year-old parents are still trying to tell them what to do. Chances are, although the patterns were established when children were very young, they became set in concrete when the children were adolescents and the parents tried to exert control over them "for their own good." While there may be real love between the generations, there is also conflict. And when the parent dies, the son or daughter, who truly loved and will miss the parent, will also be consumed with guilt for having struggled with them for so many years.

Our job as parents is to raise our children and then let go. New-borns are helpless, and our control over them is total. The only protest they can register is to wail in anger or frustration. As they develop, they begin to explore their world. Then we begin to learn to let go—to allow them to fall down, to learn that certain things are hot or cold or slick or deep. We hover anxiously, concerned for their safety. We say, "Don't climb the stairs, you might fall," and the moment we turn our backs, they start to climb them again. We say, "Don't put tiny objects in your mouth, you could choke," but everything they find on the floor goes in their mouths.

All along the way we learn to compromise with them. They are almost always a step ahead of us, demanding what we're not quite ready to give: to pick out their own clothes, to sleep all night in the backyard, to decide which vegetables they will and will not eat. By the time they become adolescents, we've been through scraped knees, learning to cross the street alone, learning to swim in the deep end of the pool, learning how and when to call 911, and learning to stay home alone for short periods of time.

The tests keep coming. In adolescence the desire to grow up seems to shift into high gear. It's as though they can't wait. Girls want to wear makeup, get their ears pierced, replace glasses with contacts, wear bras. Boys want to shave, stay out late, borrow the family car. Both of them may start to swear, to smoke, to experiment with drugs or alcohol, to try skipping school, to attempt shoplifting.

Their first sexual encounter may be just one more item on the checklist. But because it can be so difficult to talk about, because of the way we were raised and our belief that it is an adult activity, because we parents are often so unsure how we feel about it, and because today it can have very serious health consequences, sex is often the most problematic of them all.

Parents with young children who know what's ahead can start early to lay the groundwork of trust and communication that will make this process easier during the difficult teen years.

Parents of teenagers may need to back up and start with that apology: "Lisa, this is hard for me, but I want to talk to you about sex. I'm sorry I didn't do this a long time ago with you, but it's very embarrassing for me because Grandma and Grandpa never talked to me about sex. I know it's hard for you, too. Please forgive me for my silence these past years and let's start over."

As we relinquish control along the way, we are still important to our children. We can be helper, friend, advocate, confidant, and adviser. As long as our children live under our roof, we can still set reasonable rules. (For example, we might say fill the gas tank after you borrow the car, separate bedrooms for sleep-over guests, respect our comfort level in the way you behave in our house, do your own dishes, and so forth.) But we have less control over their minds and bodies, and we are kidding ourselves if we think it can be any other way.

The teenagers we talked to about sex said their advice to their parents would be: Be open, tell us the truth, and give us honest information. Love us and support us. They also said two other things that are very important:

1. Don't judge us.
2. Give us guidance.

Our best bet—our *only* bet—is to teach them to be responsible. To teach them to protect themselves. If we really love them and care about their well-being, we should let them know how to have emotionally and physically satisfying sex lives, either by discussing this with them or by pointing them to the books and people that will tell them.

As sexually experienced adults, we parents know that sex is most emotionally satisfying when it's part of a loving relationship and not a routine part of the dating ritual. We feel that casual sex not only cheapens the act but also makes the actors feel cheap—whatever their ages.

In terms of physical satisfaction, we want them to know that "Wham, bam, thank you, ma'am" is not a formula for good sex. He may like it, but she's not going to get much out of it. She's going to feel used. After a while he's going to find it an empty experience as well, and he isn't going to feel very good about himself.

We don't have to teach our teenagers technique. That may be too much for some of us. Books and videos are available, and we can tell our teens that, but we must also tell them that the best way to enjoy sex is through honest communication between the couple. They should know that they have a responsibility to themselves and to their partner to know that there is sex and there is lovemaking, that the two of them are very different, and that when sexual intercourse is part of an enduring relationship, making love is infinitely more satisfying than having sex.

When the two of us began this quest to come to terms with our teenage daughter's sexual activity, we found it difficult to accept that she had made up her own mind about whether and when to be sexually active. Perhaps we had influenced that decision, but we did not control it. Ultimately it had little or nothing to do with us. Alex was her own person and she made her own decisions. That was that.

As Dennis Dailey told us, parents have to understand that the desire for sex is not only normal, but necessary and right. We are all sexual, from birth until death. At some point our children will choose to express their need and desire for sexual relations. The decision is out of our hands.

What parents can do is to help to assure that their teens make good choices and decisions regarding sex. Dennis Dailey says that partners are ready for sex if each of them is comfortable with their level of involvement and feels no guilt; if neither of them is pressuring the other for sex; and if both feel certain their reputation will not be compromised and they will not be humiliated.

Dr. Dailey says partners are not ready if either is using sex to prove maturity, worth, or rebellion, or to attract the other. They are not ready if they cannot discuss and agree upon methods of contraception, if they cannot discuss STDs, and if they cannot discuss and agree upon what happens if contraception fails.

The ability to meet those conditions is not determined by age. *There is no magic age* for when sex becomes appropriate. Unfortunately, couples don't have to take a test before they have sex. As we've said before, education is the only answer.

Just before Alex's return from New York, we had a long conversation with her on the phone. We told her that we'd been going through a lot of soul searching, that we'd taken ourselves back in time to when we were teenagers in order to understand her feelings better. We apologized for having made her life, Marissa's, and ours so unpleasant over the issue of sex. "For many reasons we didn't like your boyfriend, but our focus on sex kept us from dealing rationally with you on the other reasons. Sex isn't the only reason we were upset about him, but we know you thought it was," we said.

She expressed curiosity about our trip back in time and said she looked forward to hearing about it. "I always wondered what you guys were like," she said dryly. "I figured you were born full-grown."

She was surprised to hear us not only being reasonable but actually apologizing, too. "That's okay," she quickly replied. She sounded mature beyond her years. "You were just doing what you thought you should."

"You know," we said, "it would be helpful to us to hear your thoughts about everything that happened this last year. Would you be willing to write them down for us, to reflect on what was going on in your life, how the issue of sex affected it, and how you reacted to the way we responded to you?"

"I will," she said without hesitation. "I'll do it tonight and mail it to you."

"Have you been hearing from the Boyfriend?" we asked as casually as possible.

Her voice was guarded. "Not lately. But I'm having a good time. I went to the beach yesterday with Clay. He's just a friend," she added quickly.

On the other end of the line, here in Kansas, we smiled knowingly at each other.

She really did sit down that night and write us. Here's an excerpt from her long letter:

I was attracted to my old boyfriend because he was a challenge. He did what he wanted and wasn't tied down to silly
curfews and commitments like I was. It didn't bother me that
he used drugs and had a not-so-hot past and wasn't close to
his family, because we had fun when we were together.

Several months into the relationship he began to change.
He was rude and demanding and put down my friends. He
tried to get me to do things he knew would upset you (like
drive to Mexico with him—I didn't tell you that) but somehow I kept my head. I was always on edge and began to lose
my closeness with you. You were the boss, the law, the jail
keepers, the parents.

The sex factor made it harder. You always said sex was to
be saved for someone you love. I didn't think that meant you
couldn't care that way about someone until you were married. I felt it was my body, my conscience, and my responsibility, not yours. But as soon as you found out, you acted like
it was your body, your responsibility, and definitely your conscience. You always said I could talk to you about sex, but I
knew if I tried, you would flip. I knew you weren't there for
me.

So I did what anyone would do—I packed up my feelings
and emotions. You wouldn't give an inch, so I just decided
to stop caring about anything and to look the way I wanted,
eat what I wanted, and live the way I wanted.

You thought the only way for things to get better was for
me to go back to being an innocent 14-year-old. But people

change. I wanted to have the freedom of an adult. I felt more mature than the kids around me. I wanted to find out what kind of person I was. I didn't like living with parents who thought they could pull strings to make my legs or arms move. Since you wouldn't let me grow up, I cut the strings and proceeded to find things out for myself. I wanted to live a little dangerously and feel and experience and learn so I could understand things. You tried to hold me back. You were the ones who were supposed to be on my side, but I felt like you were against me.

And it was all because of sex—a little word that can make a person feel like a zillion dollars. Sex is in our human nature. Who has the right to tell another person that they cannot have sex? Parents should explain and share their ideas, views, and morals. They have the right to be upset and disappointed, but I don't think that gives them the right to put an age or date on this.

Parents always tell their kids, "Don't do this, you're not allowed to do that," and most kids do it all anyway just to find out why it was forbidden. Maybe if it was explained instead of forbidden there would be less conflict and more love and understanding.

I dated my old boyfriend for eight long months. When I came here to New York, no one knew about all the problems. I felt released, like I could start over. I've been able to come to an understanding about what happened this last year and it's time to move on.

So I want you to know—that I've fallen in love with Clay! I couldn't be happier. We know long-distance relationships are hard, but we don't think it'll be a problem. He wants to come visit us in Kansas this fall. He's a good person, very caring and respectful. In a way, he saved me from my-

self. He's the one who heard me when I talked and gave me
feedback that helped me. No games, no wars, no constant
verbal battles, just understanding and commitment. I feel free
emotionally and I am at peace.

I'd like to keep a strong relationship with you. But I need
to be my own person. How you judge me means a lot to me.
I have let go of the past and am ready for a fresh start. I hope
you will be happy for me. See you in a few days.

Love,
Alex

Letting go when it's time. That's an important part of the job
description of a parent. And communicating our thoughts and feelings
is part of the job description of healthy families.

In the few months before Alex dated the Boyfriend and while she
was going out with him, we were in a power struggle. She pushed
and we pulled. Communication was superficial. We lectured and
took away privileges and joked and got angry. We didn't ask her how
she felt about anything, although we were quick to tell her how we
felt. We expected her to feel the same way and to act according to
our wishes. The more we tried to control, the harder she had to fight
for her autonomy. We had an image of what we wanted her to be,
and we certainly didn't want her to be sexually active at so young an
age. But her image was different and she was determined to be her
own person. Her letter made that clear to us. She had been able to
write what she had not said to us—or if she had, we hadn't heard it.
But in reading it, we did and we were touched by it. We were sixteen
again, searching, fighting our parents for our independence, and
feeling as if we were throwing pebbles at a brick wall. No wonder we

had poor communication with our daughter: we didn't listen to her any better than our parents had listened to us.

If we could do it over again, we'd try to do four things:

1. Communicate more openly and honestly with her from an earlier age.
2. Make sure she had some skill in how to decide whether sex was right for the relationship.
3. Make sure she had the information she needed to protect herself and her partner physically.
4. Try to keep lines of communication open so we could help her when she wanted it and could help her to view us as her allies and advocates.

We have wondered how we would have reacted to her becoming sexually active had we liked the Boyfriend better. It's a moot point. We did the best we could at the time, and we think she knows that and accepts our apology for what we wish we had done differently.

In the best of all possible worlds, families would be grounded in a mutual respect that would allow teens to come to their parents— their advocates—with their questions, their fears, and their problems, knowing their parents would tell them the truth, help them, and love them no matter what. The teens would know that they were held accountable for their behavior, and they would know and accept the consequences of their behavior.

Along the way we would tell them the truth about life—that it isn't a bed of roses, that actions involve consequences, that school can be difficult but they don't have the right to skip it, that part-time jobs can be boring but they don't have the right to quit or to talk back to the boss, that marriage can be wonderful but it's also very hard work, that having a baby is a miracle but babies are expensive, noisy, and self-centered.

We need to tell them that sex can be very pleasurable and lots of fun but if used wrongly has the potential of being ugly, exploitative, and dangerous. Few of us actually think our kids might make it to their wedding nights as virgins. To tell them "Just say no" is to skirt our responsibilities as parents. We must be their primary teachers. We cannot rely on anyone else to do this. We must think of sex-education courses as only an adjunct. Few of them attempt to teach values. That's *our* job. When we are helping our children form their values about sex, we should explain to them that all of us must make choices about how we will handle our sex lives. Abstinence is one choice. It's a very good choice, especially in this day of disease. But if we frighten them into abstinence by telling them they will go to hell or get AIDS and die a terrible death, what we are doing is assuring that they will become sexually dysfunctional adults.

If we say, "I think you're too young to have sex," or "I don't think you should have sex yet," we need to follow up with, "Here's why." The only realistic way to complete that conversation is to say, "I know I can't make this decision for you. I hope you wait, but if you do choose to have sex, here are some important things I think you should consider." Then follow up with realistic information about birth control and the emotional consequences that go along with having sex.

It can be frightening to have to put so much trust in young people, who can be so flighty and flippant, who still pass notes in class and snap towels at each other in the locker room. But most of them will respond with some signs of maturity and responsibility if we adults do our jobs well.

One tremendous way we can help our teenagers is to arm them with knowledge about sexual exploitation: date rape, sexual harassment, lines guys use to try to get girls to have sex with them, fears of sexual inadequacy, and choices they must make about their reputations if they are sexually active, along with the information they need on birth control, STDs, and how to take care of the sexually active teenage body. So many topics need covering: masturbation, disease, pregnancy, values, and pleasure. That last one is tough when we don't want our teens to be sexually active, but it, too, needs to be discussed. They need to know how good sex can be so they'll have something to compare their experiences with.

With teens like our daughter Marissa who are taking things at a slower, easier pace, we can relate in a different way, but it's important that we not think we don't need to be doing anything. She needs input too. She needs encouragement and support for her decision to wait to become sexually active, because she may be feeling pressured by boys and even by girlfriends who want her to be doing what they are doing. We need to let her know we support her decision.

Finally, we need to remember that teenagers need physical affection from us, they need our trust, and they need to know we love them. Too many teenagers think their parents provide for them because they *have* to, not because they want to.

But they need to understand that loving them doesn't mean we'll rescue them when they do wrong. It means we love them enough to let them learn from their mistakes.

It means being open and receptive to their thoughts and feelings so they can come to us with any concern.

It means we let them know often that we think they're special and we're glad they're ours.

And then—because this is what parenting is all about—with the safety net of our love and caring in place under them, we continue to step aside and let them experience life.

APPENDIX A

SHARING INFORMATION
ABOUT SEX AND SEXUALITY WITH
CHILDREN AND TEENS

Basing our recommendations on our study, our discussions with adolescents and adults, and our interviews with experts, we're going to suggest some broad approaches for parents who want to share information about sex and sexuality with their children and teenagers.

In Appendix C we've listed resources we recommend for more in-depth information. What follows here will get you started.

Ideally, children will receive their sex and sexuality education from both parents in a consistent fashion starting at birth and continuing into young adulthood.

When spouses or ex-spouses differ and compromises can't be reached, we suggest each parent make it clear to the child that his or her own belief is being expressed. This must be done without devaluing, undercutting, or criticizing the other parent's beliefs. It doesn't hurt children to know there is more than one opinion about issues. When this happens, urge your child to make the choice that seems best for him or her.

Always try, beginning when your child is old enough to talk, to answer questions in a straightforward, nonjudgmental way. If at all possible, leave words like "sin," "dirty," "bad," and "wrong" out of your vocabulary. Use anatomically correct names whenever possible.

Children and adolescents crave honesty, and they need to know that adults they trust with their concerns will treat them with dignity and respect. In like manner, teach them to respect your privacy, just as you will theirs. Privacy is important to our well-being.

If any question embarrasses you, don't be afraid to acknowledge this, and then answer it the very best way you can, even if your hands are shaking and your voice is quavering. You are laying groundwork that will be invaluable in the teenage years. For example, if you can talk casually and naturally about menstruation early on, it will be much easier for you and your daughter when it's time to prepare her for it.

Sexuality in Children

Remember that sexuality does not kick in at puberty. We are all born sexual. Sex is not something boys are more interested in than girls. Needs and expression are different, but interest is high in both sexes.

Sonograms of babies in the womb sometimes show males with erections. Studies have established that male fetuses have erections approximately every ninety minutes. (So do adult males during sleep.)

When infants touch their genitals, they discover that contact with the genitals feels good. How you react is as important as what you say when this happens. If you push the child's hand away or act alarmed, you're delivering the message that the feel-good feelings of sexuality are wrong.

Normal Curiosity

We suggest that touching and self-exploration be considered normal. If we treat them as something wrong, we are once again instilling guilt in our children for what is a natural activity. When the child begins pointing to body parts and asking for names, give them openly and correctly.

What children must learn from an early age is that masturbation— a normal activity most children engage in—and touching the genitals are okay, but that they are something you do in private. It's important that you react casually to masturbation. Help your children learn the importance of privacy for this, just as they learn to close the door when they use the bathroom, or just as they learn they must not hit other children or throw toys in the house or use inappropriate language.

Sex Play in Children

When they transfer their curiosity to playmates and "play doctor," the parents' role is not to stop but to monitor to be certain no one is getting hurt. Children must know, for example, that they cannot insert anything into their own or another's body. Most parents are quite uptight about childhood sex play, and if your child is engaging in this with children of friends or neighbors, you may want to discuss it with the other parents to be certain no one gets unduly upset by it. This is a touchy subject in our culture, and other parents' feelings must be respected.

Educating About Sexual Abuse

This is the time to begin teaching your children about respect for the body and what is proper touch and what is not. They must know that not only is no adult to touch their genitals, but if one does, no matter what promises or threats might be made, they are to tell you or another responsible adult immediately—and without fear that you will become angry or blame them.

Teach your children that if approached by an older child or an adult to do something they know they shouldn't do, they should state clearly and loudly, "No!" and "Stop!" and then leave and go tell a trusted adult what happened.

According to national studies, one of every three girls and one of every five boys suffer some form of sexual abuse before the age of eighteen. The offender is someone known and trusted by the child in 80 to 90 percent of documented cases. No families—regardless of race, religion, culture, or socioeconomic background—are exempt.

Learning Sex Roles

Young children explore sex roles and learn how to be male or female in our culture. Little boys want to be like Daddy. Little girls want to dress up in Mommy's clothes and mimic her activities. For a couple of years boys and girls may still enjoy playing together, but this ends by age eight or so, and girls stick with girls, boys with boys.

These years are also the time to lay the groundwork for how males and females should relate to each other—that neither has the right to harass the other sexually with comments about his or her body or to expect sexual favors in return for any kind of assistance, and that adults have no right to do these things to children.

Don't assume your child doesn't know about sex. An average ten-year-old reportedly sees 9,000 scenes suggesting intercourse or making reference to it in a year of television watching, and 93 percent of sexual encounters on television are between unmarried characters, so they aren't going to believe you if you say sex is something only married people do.

When situations arise in the movies and on television that present women as victims or show violent, coercive, or unprotected sex, parents should counteract the show's message through honest dialogue with the child. This doesn't mean preaching your position to them. They won't hear that. It means engaging them in conversation about what they saw and what they think about it, followed by what you think about it. It's a good time to get them thinking about smoking, alcohol, and drug usage and how and why to say no to them.

One of the most difficult messages to get across to children and young people is that bad things can happen, and that an attitude of "It won't happen to me" can be fatal. At the same time, you don't want to fill them so full of fears that they can't function. Balance your earnings with "If you are cautious, you should be safe." This approach can apply to teaching them swimming safety and how to protect themselves from AIDS—and everything in between.

Your maturing son or daughter is going to start wanting increasingly grown-up privileges, and you may want to establish some markers. For example, depending on what goes on where you live, you might tell your daughter she can get her ears pierced when she's ten and start wearing pale nail polish at eleven.

By age eleven both boys and girls are interested in the particulars of sexual intercourse. They may also get involved in group "show and tell" with same-sex friends. Girls display their budding breasts and boys may be involved with group masturbation.

Girls eleven to fifteen may start trying out their sexuality on their father, touching his hair, perhaps, or wanting to fix his food—intimate acts that they see their mothers do. Moms and dads often get confused about this. Mothers may react to the child as a rival. Fathers may actually find themselves sexually attracted to their daughters. Try to remember that girls are "practicing" on the safest male in their lives—the one they can trust above all others not to take advantage of them. This behavior will pass, so try to be patient. If it's really bothersome and you feel the need to say something, do it in such a way that you do not humiliate your daughter.

Sex Education

By age ten, boys need to know about "wet dreams" and that they are normal, so that when they occur, they will accept them as natural.

By age nine, young though it may seem to you, girls should know about menstruation and how their bodies are going to change. Parents can provide this information—particularly moms, since girls find it more embarrassing to talk with their fathers about such matters even if they have a strong, close relationship. Or see to it that your daughter attends a good course sponsored by a hospital, community agency, school, or church.

We strongly encourage fathers to be involved in their daughters' sex education. It will allow fathers to be closer to their daughters both as teenagers and adults.

Ongoing Parental Involvement

Do not assume that because your son or daughter has attended a sex-education course your job is done. Far from it. As you know from reading this book, teaching your children about sex and sexuality is an ongoing process. You're just getting ready to move into the heavy stuff!

With the basic information in place—what intercourse is, how it happens, how babies develop in the womb and are born—your children still need a great deal of information. They need to know that sex can be dangerous, that it can lead to AIDS and other STDs as well as pregnancy, *but* that sex is also pleasurable and that the important thing is to handle it responsibly. You'll want to come back to this groundwork you are establishing many times as your child enters the teen years.

Managing Personal Hygiene

Girls should be given an assortment of types of personal-hygiene products so they can experiment and find what they like best. Again, this should be treated in a straightforward manner so that girls aren't embarrassed to tell their mothers when they need supplies replenished.

One of the most important messages that should be relayed to both boys and girls is that sexual development varies widely and that it's all normal. Girls may start their periods anytime between ages nine and sixteen, and all of that is normal.

As soon as breast development begins, girls should start wearing bras so they won't feel self-conscious. Most girls are anxious to wear them and don't have to be pushed to do so.

Puberty

In some households this stage of development goes smoothly, and in some it wreaks havoc. All children are not the same. Accept that. You're going to need patience, vigilance, and a sense of humor for a number of years so that you and your children get through this in a happy, healthy manner.

One of the most serious side effects of puberty can be that girls' self-esteem plunges. They might have been academic stars in elementary school, and now teachers don't call on them as much and boys seem to get all the attention. They may be self-conscious about their developing bodies and breast size. They may be highly sensitive to teasing or criticism. Both sexes worry about height, weight, body hair, acne, and hair styles. Boys' voices begin to change, lowering in pitch, only to flare embarrassingly into a higher register—again unexpectedly. Both sexes can get painful crushes on movie and singing idols, teachers, or their best friend's parent.

By seventh grade, you should be talking openly and frequently with your son or daughter about sex. Their classmates will begin to lose their virginity now, and while your goal will probably be to help your child delay this experience as long as possible, don't put your head in the sand and assume that because you told them to wait, they will.

The Parent as Teacher

It may embarrass you and your teenager, but it's time to buy an assortment of items associated with safer sex—latex condoms lubricated with the spermicide nonoxynol-9, or latex condoms and the spermicide separately—and show your teen how to use them. In doing so, you are saying you realize that sooner or later they may choose to engage in sexual intercourse and you want them to be as protected as possible.

Emphasize to them that in spite of what their friends may tell them, you *can* get pregnant the first time, during your period, using withdrawal, standing up, or while on drugs. It's also important that they know that condoms can fail. In tests, the breakage rate can run 20 percent. Boys and girls should know that condoms have expiration dates that must be followed; that condom wrappers must be opened carefully to prevent tearing or stretching; that air bubbles should be squeezed out of the tip of the condom to prevent pressure that can result in breakage; that oil-based lubricants like lotions, oils, or petroleum jelly can weaken latex condoms; and that a condom should *never* be used more than once. Remind your son or daughter that only latex condoms provide effective barriers to the AIDS virus.

Help both sons and daughters to recognize the lines they may hear ("You'd do it with me if you really loved me," and so forth) and how to respond to them ("If you really loved me, you wouldn't pressure me"). Learning to resist destructive peer pressure is very difficult for adolescents. You can help by going through a series of role-playing scenarios with them. They may seem uncooperative at the time, but you are banking that they will remember the message when they need it.

Be sensitive to how difficult young love is, and that when they suffer heartache, it's very real. Respect it—don't diminish it, or your child will not trust you with information about his or her feelings.

Teach your son that when a girl says no, he must stop whatever he is doing. Boys are pressured in our culture to chalk up the number of girls they've had sex with. We must firmly deliver the message that "scoring" is not right, that sex should be part of a loving, caring relationship requiring that they be sensitive and protective toward their partner. We must reinforce the message that having sex does not prove manliness, nor does having sex with multiple partners.

Teach your daughter that she must be careful not to put herself in a vulnerable position where she may have sex forced upon her. Suggestive clothing and heavy makeup, going into an isolated area with a young man, or having too much to drink all put her at extra risk. It's unfair to females, but this is how it is.

If you suspect your son or daughter is in conflict over his or her sexual orientation, try to remain open and available for discussion and assistance. A sympathetic professional with experience in gender-orientation issues can help you both deal with this issue.

Remember that you can't control your child's sex life. Your job now is to be an adviser and a guide. The example you set is important. The desire for sexual expression is a normal, natural part of life. Yes, sex can be dangerous. It can also be pleasurable. Our children need to know both.

APPENDIX B

COMMUNICATING WITH TEENS ABOUT SEX AND SEXUALITY

Being our children's sex educators is a relatively new role for American parents. In the past very few parents did much beyond the "birds and the bees" lecture. Chastity was the expectation, especially for females. Women went to their bridal bed expecting to be "taught" by husbands who usually had very little, if any, experience. Somehow they muddled through—some with good results and many not—and they raised their children the same way they had been raised: with ignorance.

All of us are afraid that if we talk frankly with our children about sex and sexuality, they will think we condone sexual activity. Studies prove that children and teenagers will become sexually active with or without parental permission.

Many families use fear to control their children's sexual involvement. But fear—of being ostracized from the family, of pregnancy, of disease—may not prevent sexual activity, and it may very well create sexual dysfunction.

We believe children who have been raised with a healthy attitude toward sex—that it is a natural part of life as opposed to something that is secretive and dirty—will be better sexually adjusted, and certainly happier throughout their lives, no matter when or if they decide to become sexually active. As loving parents, we should want this for our children.

We know that communicating with adolescents and preadolescents about sex and sexuality *will not* cause them to become sexually active, nor will it increase their sexual activity. On the contrary, it will lessen their fears, correct misconceptions, and help them to make better decisions. With good education and parental support they are more likely to delay sexual involvement and to protect themselves when they begin. The older children get, the less they want to talk to their parents about sex. Therefore, the sooner this is started the better.

What follows are some tips on how to establish and maintain communication with children on sex and sexuality. In Appendix C you will find a list of resources we recommend for more information.

1. *Accept the task of sex educator.* We know from the young people we have visited with that they *want* information about sex and sexuality from parents. They trust parents to give them the truth. Most of them know they can't rely on friends and the media. If both parents are present in the household, they need the input of both points of view. Don't worry if this is not the case. One parent can do very well. What's important is that parent and child are communicating on this subject.

Don't rely on the school or community to handle this task for you. Most courses teach only biological facts and don't address values, options, and relationships. You can supplement what your child learns in classes, and you can attend a class together and use this as a starting point.

One college student who has herpes told us she wished her parents had told her something about the disease. She knew nothing about it when she contracted it and feels it has all but ruined her sex life. "How do you tell a guy you've got it?" she asked. "The moment you mention it, even if you're being very careful and you can't infect them at that time, they suddenly cool and that's the last you see of them. At this rate, I'll *never* get married because I'll never develop a close relationship with a guy."

2. *Become knowledgeable about sex and sexuality.* Maybe you know all you need to. If not, read up on birth control, sexually transmitted diseases, and other topics you'll want to discuss with your child. Show as well as tell. When the time is right, purchase different types of birth-control devices and discuss each of them. Demonstrate how to unwrap a condom—provided you know how. Or make sure your child will get this information some other way.

Focus on sex and sexuality as normal and natural. Don't use negative words like "dirty," "bad," or "wrong" when discussing sex. For example, if the topic of homosexuality comes up, if your beliefs will allow you to, try to explain this as a form of sexuality that is natural to a portion of the population.

3. *Accept that it may be awkward and embarrassing to talk to your child about sex—and then do it anyway.* If you actually say, "This is embarrassing for me because my parents never talked to me about sex," you and your child will probably both relax and do just fine. If you don't say something and you stumble through whatever it is you want to say, your kid may not hear anything and will instead remember only the embarrassment.

Children may be embarrassed, but they're also curious and they want the information. If they protest that they don't need to hear about sex because they don't have sex lives, say something like, "I know you may not feel you're ready for this information, but I'd like to share it with you now so that if you do need it, or a friend of yours needs it, you'll know the facts."

If they tell you they already know all about it, try to engage them in a give-and-take discussion to find out just what they do know. Ask them to explain something to you. Compliment them when they have the information, and gently correct them when they have something wrong.

If you learn your child is sexually active and you disapprove, try to say something like, "We would prefer that you wait. However, if you make the decision to go ahead, here are some things we hope you will consider so you will be safe."

4. *Along with facts, talk about feelings, relationships, and how the other person is affected. And don't forget to discuss consequences!* This is the stuff kids rarely get in sex-education courses. If, early on, our children learn to take into account how what they are doing affects a partner, they may cause far less hurt and do fewer things they will regret. They are also more likely to have sexually healthy and happy relationships.

When an opportunity arises to discuss consequences, use it. Teens often have very mistaken notions of how their parents will react to bad news. For example, a fourteen-year-old girl may think her parents would kick her out were she to get pregnant. That thought may torment her if indeed she thinks she might be pregnant. She may settle for desperate means such as running away or an illegal abortion to save herself from her parents' wrath and end up in far greater trouble.

5. *Apologize if you are starting late, or if you change your views on something.* We believe Dennis Dailey and other experts on families and sexuality are right when they recommend this technique. Children are very forgiving. They will appreciate your willingness to admit

a mistake and correct it and will learn a valuable lesson they may use many times in their lives when *they* make mistakes.

6. *Set up a resource center in your home where your children can get more information.* There are some topics many of us don't feel comfortable discussing with our children, and the children don't want to discuss them, either. But if children have access to age-appropriate books that tell them what they need to know, they *will* read them. Suggestions are in Appendix C.

7. *When your children ask you a question, answer it directly and honestly, and without judgment.* It may be something like "How do lesbians make love?" and it may be "How old were you when you did it for the first time?" If you respond by saying, "You have a dirty mind," or "That's none of your business," you're shutting down communication. They'll stop viewing you as their source of honest, unbiased information. To do this task well, you've got to be ready for tough questions and prepared to answer honestly. If you don't know the answer to a question, say so and tell your children you'll find out and get back to them. Then *do* it.

8. *Take advantage of those moments that arise when you can share your views.* It may be while watching a television show. Your kids see ten to twelve sex scenes a week on television if they are average American teenagers, who watch 23,000 hours of TV by the age of twenty. Take advantage of television as a teaching tool to discuss such topics as sexual harassment, date rape, and sex outside of marriage.

9. *Teach yourself to not talk down to your child.* When children are younger, we probably all do this to a degree. It can be a tough habit to break as they get older, but we must do it if we want to communicate with them effectively. As children mature, it's more imperative than

ever that we talk *with* them, not *to* them. Teenagers say they want to be treated as equals when discussing sex and sexuality. This is tough for parents, but it's worth striving for. If we can't treat them as equals, we can at least show respect for their viewpoints. Listen quietly and thoughtfully. Discuss options without arguing.

10. *Communicate your values without apology—and expect them to be challenged.* Teenagers are trying to find out who and what they are. They are also trying to separate from us. They *want* to be independent from us and have their own identities. We want that, too! Sometimes they will do or say outlandish things to show us they are individuals. When this acting-out involves sex and sexuality, we must continue to say what we believe and to model it in our own lives. We're going to get told we're old-fashioned or out of it. All teenagers do that to their parents—we probably did it to our own, at least behind their backs. We should not take this personally.

11. *Give up trying to control your teen's actions. You can't win this one.* Getting angry, making threats, condemning, ridiculing, or making life generally intolerable for teenagers in an attempt to keep them from being sexually active won't work. It just makes teens secretive and creates conflict in the family. Instead our goal must be to teach our teens to be *responsible* for their actions and to understand that actions often have undesirable consequences.

11. *Recognize that you may indeed not understand what your teen is going through.* When we say, "Just say no," or "If your friends suggest doing something wrong, just leave and come home," we're forgetting how difficult peer pressure is and we're not recognizing that our teens' world *is* different from what ours was. Teens deal with a lot more pressures than we did. If you've got your head in the sand, pull it out! Find out what's really going on or you can't be helpful

to your child. Talk with other parents, teens, and teachers. Get a feel for what teen life is like today.

12. *Express your appreciation of how tough it is to be a teen.* If you can find ways to compliment your teens by noticing the good they do instead of just remarking on the negative, if you can bolster their self-esteem and help them solve whatever difficulties they are up against—even at times when you can't stand them—you are more likely to maintain (or develop) a close, loving relationship with them.

One way to foster this is to set aside time to do normal, routine things with your teen: Go to lunch together, see a show or movie, take walks or drives.

Along with this, try to have some physical contact with your teen. A pat on the back, a spontaneous hug, a kiss goodnight if they're willing can melt hard feelings and build bridges between you and your child. The hug you give them may well be the only one they get that day, and all humans need loving physical contact.

13. *Try not to deliver ultimatums.* Teenagers can be very difficult to live with. Your teen needs to know that you are flexible enough to believe there are two sides to every issue. If you've made a statement like "Homosexuality is a sin," you may be setting your child up for a life of pain and secrecy. Assure your children regularly that you may not always like or approve of their actions but that you'll always love them, unconditionally, and you will never abandon them.

Handing down judgments won't work. If parents say something like "If I ever learn that you're messing around with a boy, young lady, I'm going to take a switch to you" (or "lock you in your room," or "send you to live with your grandmother," or "take away your car"), teenagers will find a way, as we've said before, to continue the questionable behavior—but it will be in secret and they will create a load of guilt that they will have to drag with them into adulthood.

14. *Don't compromise your values if your child becomes sexually active.* Some parents throw up their hands and figure since they can't do anything about it, they might as well look the other way. You have every right to continue to insist that sexual activity not take place in your home. Your college-age children may share an apartment with their girlfriend or boyfriend, but that doesn't mean when they come to spend the weekend they share a bedroom at your house. Children of all ages must respect their parents' comfort level. It's *your* house, and *you* set the rules. It's not your job to make your child happy. Nor should you rush to their rescue when things don't go right for them.

High school counselor Joan Jacobson gets concerned when parents think they can't handle their children's problems and fall prey to advertising for inpatient facilities for "troubled" teens.

"Parents go looking for quick fixes," she said. "In my experience, all these facilities do is redouble the problem. You put teenagers away for a while, and when they come out, they're set up for further trouble—and they always get it."

Harriet Barrish, a Kansas City psychologist who has written several books for parents along with her husband, Jay Barrish, commented: "I get the most concerned about kids who don't have anybody to talk to. I don't worry as long as they say they have someone—a sibling, a friend's mom—it doesn't matter as long as someone is there for them."

15. *Recognize that teenagers are tough on marriages—and take good care of your relationship.* Problems over sex can drive a wedge between spouses. It's helpful to talk out the "what ifs" before they happen so you will have a united voice, but this isn't always possible. It's important that one parent not impose a restriction, rule, or punishment without reaching an agreement with the other parent first. So if a situation arises that calls for action, tell your son or daughter you'll

get back to them after you and your husband or wife have had a chance to talk. That also gives your child time to think, and everybody can regroup later without anger. If you and your spouse simply can't agree on something serious, you may need some help from a professional. View getting professional help as a strength rather than a weakness. Family counseling with your child can also be very valuable. A good therapist will help both you and your spouse and child, or you and your child, separate fact from emotion and help you navigate turbulent waters during the teen years.

Dr. Barrish emphasizes the importance of parental communication. When she begins counseling with a family, one of her goals is to get the parents communicating with each other. Sometimes it takes several sessions.

When parents cannot agree or only one parent is in the home, it's up to the parent who is present or who can best communicate with the teen to negotiate accountability. When parents can't manage this, someone else—a trusted friend or relative, a teacher—needs to step in to help. Teens who are straying *need* to be accountable to someone.

16. *Help your teenager have goals and a life plan.* We all know that plans sometimes don't work out. Our experience with teens and parents has shown us that the teenager who is drifting, who has too much free time and too little supervision, and who has no goals is the one more likely to get into all kinds of trouble, including early, unprotected sex. Many teenagers have little contact with their parents, too much spending money, and no jobs, activities, or interests of their own.

Parents can insist on a part-time job and school activities. Family outings and events—a baseball game, a trip to see the grandparents, even cleaning the attic—not only promote closeness but also provide opportunities for those spontaneous talks that can be so valuable for parents and teenagers.

As difficult as it sometimes is, we encourage parents to work with teens to give them varied experiences and help them establish short-term and long-term goals.

17. *Remember that this won't last forever!* Because it won't. Teen-agers *do* grow up, and helping them to have a healthy attitude about sex and to be comfortable with their own sexuality will go far in assuring that they will be happy, productive adults.

Ideally parents should begin early to talk to children about sex and sexuality. But if they haven't, they can begin at any point to practice effective communication with their children and still achieve positive results.

Here are several situations parents may find themselves in, along with possible reactions:

You come home from work and hear giggles in your son's bed-room. You open the door (without knocking) and—surprise! There's your sixteen-year-old son and his girlfriend, sans clothes, in bed. You scream at them and force her to wrap a sheet around herself and go into the bathroom while you continue to scream at your son. You throw her clothes through the bathroom door at her, and continue ranting at your son until she leaves the house.

Have you guaranteed that this won't happen again? Perhaps. They will at least be much more careful not to get caught if they do it again. You've also guaranteed other things: (a) that you've thoroughly embarrassed your son, and while he knew better than to do what he did, he's not going to forgive you for that; (b) that he won't be talking to you about sexual matters in any shape or form; (c) that both he and the girl will take into adulthood this humiliating experience; (d) that he won't be bringing the girl to the house anymore in your presence because she will refuse to come; (e) that the girl may break up with him, in which case your son will view you as the "enemy."

"Well," you may say, "this is *my* house and I won't stand for that kind of behavior! How dare my son do that to me!"

Remember that (a) he wasn't doing it "to you." He was with his girlfriend in the private space of his bedroom, the place he considers his; (b) if you react in anger, you may never have the opportunity to think through what happened and how you want to react in the event you decide you should have done something differently.

And what could you have done? Think about this: For starters, you really shouldn't have opened the door. With strong suspicion about what was happening, if you had knocked on the door, you would have stopped it. Then you could have asked your son to come to the kitchen (or wherever) to visit with you. When he arrived, you could have, as calmly as possible, inquired about his activities and suggested that you would like his girlfriend to leave so the two of you could talk about the situation.

Once he's alone and you are able to calm down, you have the perfect opening to talk with him about entertaining his girlfriend behind a closed bedroom door and to point out that this goes against your house policy. Whether or not you've done it before, talk with him about sex and about protection. See if they are acting responsibly. A question such as "What are you using for protection?" is appropriate. Explain to him that while it is his room, house rules take precedence. Don't lecture—it won't do any good. Ask for his cooperation.

Remember, you're not going to change whether or not your son has sex—unless you scare him sexless through fear of disease or pregnancy. If you do that, you introduce all sorts of problems for him. By *not* humiliating him or his girlfriend, you have kept the channels of communication open. They will respect you and thank you for allowing them their dignity when caught in a compromising situation.

Here's another. You overhear your fifteen-year-old daughter telling a girlfriend on the phone that she plans to have sex with her boyfriend that night. What do you do?

A. Storm in, grab the phone, shout, "Oh no you're *not! You're not leaving this house, young lady, and what's more, you're grounded!*" or:

B. Create some private time with her. Explain that you weren't eavesdropping but you overheard the conversation and you're concerned. Then express your concerns and give her a chance to respond without your moralizing or nagging at her. You need honest give-and-take if she's going to actually listen to you and, you hope, heed your words.

You won't get anywhere if you put your child on the defensive with statements like "You have no right to do that!" or "What would your grandmother say if she heard about this?" or "How could you do this to me!"

On the other hand, if you're successful in establishing and maintaining good communication, things may get a little rough, too. If your teenage son says something like, "Dad [or Mom], I'm seeing this girl, you know, and when we, you know, *do* it, I, well, I *come* too fast. I can't hold it and that upsets her. I don't know what to do about it."

Your son is asking if there's something wrong with him. No matter what words he uses, he's worried and he's turning to you for help as the person who will give him a straight answer.

Consider this: First take a deep breath, then say something like "What you're talking about, son, is premature ejaculation. I understand your concern and I'll try to help you. I'm going to get a book for you that will explain that what you're experiencing is perfectly normal and that there are a number of things you can try to correct it."

Or your daughter says, "Mom, when Bobby and I do it, that special thing that's supposed to happen to women never happens for me. Why not?"

The same kind of response is needed: "What you're talking about is orgasm, and it doesn't happen every time. It can take work to achieve, and you need to learn how it works for your body."

Again offer to provide her with more information. This type of answer doesn't mean you condone your teen having sexual intercourse—it means your teen can ask you anything and you will answer questions honestly. You also have the right (and, we believe, the responsibility) to state how you feel about your child having sex, as long as you don't condemn him or her.

In this day when disease is such a threat, every parent should have a conversation with their teenage children about AIDS and other STDs. You must bring this up—they may never get around to it. Assuming you don't suspect your teen is sexually active, bring it up casually with a comment like, "I hope this won't embarrass you, but I think we need to talk about all the sexually transmitted diseases that are around, especially about AIDS, so that you'll have the right information when you need it." Then, through your reading or something you give your child to read, move through a discussion. It may be fairly one-sided. If so, ask your child to repeat key ideas so you'll know whether or not he or she understands them.

APPENDIX C

FOR MORE INFORMATION

Snuggling with young children and reading age-appropriate books on sex and sexuality is a wonderful way to establish open communication with them. Be sure to ask if they have any questions and ask them what they think about what they're learning.

With pre-teens and teenagers who may be embarrassed by such an open approach, make the books available, either as gifts to them or as part of the family library, where they will have easy access to them.

Sex and Sexuality Education for Children and Teens

While children need realistic information about sex and their own sexuality, finding age-appropriate materials may be difficult. Here are our recommendations, available through bookstores if not in public libraries:

The Family Book About Sexuality, by Mary S. Calderone, M.D., and Eric W. Johnson (New York: HarperCollins, $8.95). This is a book that should be in every home library where both parents and children of all ages can have easy access to it. Dr. Calderone and Mr. Johnson are pioneer sex educators, and this book sets the standard for all others. It explains *everything* about human sexuality in easy-to-understand language.

Girls Are Girls and Boys Are Boys, by Sol Gordon, Ph.D. (New York: Prometheus Books, $9.95). Dr. Gordon, one of America's most respected sex educators, has written a short, tastefully illustrated book for children that explains the differences between the sexes and how our bodies change sexually as we grow.

Asking About Sex and Growing Up, by Joanna Cole (New York: Beech Tree Books, $4.95). This question-answer book for children ages eight and up is written in a direct style that pre-adolescents will appreciate. In addition to covering basic information about sex and sexuality, Ms. Cole addresses such topics as masturbation, homosexuality, and birth control.

In order to keep sex and sexuality casual topics—just two aspects of growing up—another book you may want for your children is *The Body and How It Works*, by Steve Parker (New York: Dorling Kindersley, Inc., $11.95). This lavishly illustrated book takes a fascinating look inside the human body and considers each of our anatomical systems, including reproduction.

Where Did I Come From?, by Peter Mayle (New York: Carol Publishing Group, $8.95). This well-known book for children explains sexual maturation, intercourse, conception, pre-birth development, and birth in terms both clever and endearing. Even orgasm is covered in an explanation that likens it to a tickle. Parents can read this book aloud to children of four and older. Both generations will enjoy the friendly illustrations.

The Sex Education Dictionary for Today's Teens and Pre-Teens, by Dr. Dean Hoch and Nancy Hoch (Pocatello, Idaho: Landmark Publishing, $12.95). The Hochs have created a straightforward text that delivers the facts in easy-to-understand language. Its dictionary format makes it easy for readers to look up terms such as *AIDS, nocturnal emission, tampon,* and *virgin.* Learning tools include crossword puzzles and word searches.

Why Love Is Not Enough, by Sol Gordon, Ph.D. (Holbrook, MA: Bob Adams, $6.95). In his usual no-nonsense approach, Dr. Gordon provides a realistic look at what it takes to make relationships and marriage work. An excellent resource for young people experimenting with life-altering choices because they are convinced their love will last forever.

Carol Cassell's book, *Straight from the Heart* (New York: Fireside Books, $7.95), is a guide for parents of teenagers that takes them through topics related to sex and romance and also rehearses with them how to answer the questions teens have. Dr. Cassell is a sex educator who works with both parents and teens.

Lynda Madaras has written three books for teens that we like. *What's Happening to My Body? Book for Boys* (New York: Newmarket Press, $9.95), for boys ages eight to fifteen, discusses puberty education, AIDS and other STDs, and what boys need to know about girls. The companion book for girls, *Lynda Madaras' Growing-Up Guide for Girls* (New York: Newmarket Press, $9.95), tells girls about their bodies, their emotions, and what they need to know about boys. Her latest book, *Lynda Madaras Talks to Teens About AIDS* (New York: Newmarket Press, $5.95), written for ages fourteen to nineteen, discusses AIDS in reassuring language and, when appropriate, with humor.

Another AIDS resource for parents is the pamphlet *How to Talk to Your Teens and Children About AIDS*, published by the National PTA and available for 20 cents a copy with a self-addressed, stamped envelope from AIDS Brochure, 700 North Rush Street, Chicago, IL 60611.

Pregnancy and Teen Parents

Facing Teenage Pregnancy: A Handbook for the Pregnant Teen, by Patricia Roles, MSW (Washington, D.C.: Child Welfare League of America, $12.95). This is a realistic sourcebook for teens, taking them from discovery to telling others, to options and their consequences.

Teenage Fathers, by Karen Gravelle and Leslie Peterson (New York: Julian Messner, $5.95). Teen fathers are often overlooked, and the authors have presented their point of view, discussing issues and relating numerous true stories, both upbeat and depressing.

Teen Parenting—Discipline from Birth to Three, by Jeanne Warren Lindsay and Sally McCullough. (Available from Morning Glory Press, 6595 San Haroldo Way, Buena Park, CA 90620, for $11.95 postage paid.) The authors, experienced in working with pregnant and parenting teens, offer realistic advice to young people on how to learn to discipline their children positively—regardless of how they themselves have been disciplined.

Teen Parents and Child Support is a pamphlet that explains how the Family Support Act affects teen parents, explains state involvement, and suggests ways to increase participation in child support by teen parents. Order from CLASP Publications, 1616 P Street N.W., Suite 450, Washington, D.C. 20036, for $5 plus $3 shipping and handling.

Homosexuality

Excellent resources about homosexuality are available for both parents and teens. Recommended reading and audio lists are available free of charge from Parents FLAG, P.O. Box 27605, Washington, D.C. 20038-7605. Enclose a self-addressed, stamped business-size envelope.

For information about Parents FLAG and the chapter nearest you, write Parents FLAG Family & Chapter Support Office, P.O. Box 20308, Denver, CO 80220.

Here are other books we particularly recommend. If you cannot get them through your library or bookstore, you may order any of them through Lambda Rising, 800-621-6969.

Beyond Acceptance, by Carolyn Griffin and Marian and Arthur Wirth (Englewood Cliffs, NJ: Prentice Hall, $9.95). In this book for parents, a group of parents of lesbians and gays speak personally of their experiences with their children.

Is the Homosexual My Neighbor?, by Letha Scanzoni and Virginia Ramey Mollenkott (New York: HarperCollins, $9.95). Homosexuality is considered from a Christian viewpoint in this classic work that argues for understanding and compassion toward homosexuals. It is written for the general reader, and biblical and theological research is presented, along with findings from the fields of psychology and sociology.

Now That You Know, by Betty Fairchild and Nancy Hayward (New York: Harcourt Brace Jovanovich, $9.95). Subtitled "What Every Parent Should Know About Homosexuality," this well-known work is for the parent who has just learned of a child's homosexuality.

One Teenager in Ten: Writings by Gay and Lesbian Youth, edited by Ann Heron (Boston: Alyson Publications, $4.95). This collection of first-person experiences offers reassurance and support to homosexual young people who may feel lonely and isolated.

Understanding Sexual Identity, by Janice E. Rench (Minneapolis: Lerner Publishing Co., $4.95). This book for gay and lesbian teens and their friends explains issues about homosexuality in easy-to-read language.

When Someone You Know Is Gay, by Susan and Daniel Cohen (New York: M. Evans and Company, $13.95). Written for anyone interested in knowing more about homosexuality, this book answers questions and concerns nongay youth and adults may have.

Homosexuality and AIDS

We strongly recommend Beverly Barbo's very moving and informative book *The Walking Wounded,* in which she tells the story of her homosexual son Tim and his death from AIDS. Order it postage paid for $12.95 from Carlson's Publishing, P.O. Box 364, Lindsborg, KS 67456-0364.

Parenting

Hundreds of books on parenting are in the bookstores. It's difficult to single out the very best, but these are our personal favorites:

John Rosemond's Six-Point Plan for Raising Happy, Healthy Children, by John Rosemond (Kansas City: Andrews and McMeel, $8.95) Rosemond helps parents change their approach from a child-centered household to a couple-centered household through a no-nonsense plan to help children grow happily *out* of their parents' lives.

Raising Self-Reliant Children in a Self-Indulgent World, by H. Stephen Glenn and Jane Nelsen (Rocklin, CA: Prima Publishing, $9.95). Glenn is well known for his parent seminars on developing capable young people, and his book explains his techniques to accomplish this.

You CAN Say NO to Your Teenager, by Shalov, Sollinger, Spotts, Steinbrecher, and Thorpe (Reading, MA: Addison-Wesley, $16.95). Five adolescent psychologists and counselors give practical advice to parents on how to handle normal parent-adolescent conflicts.

Sex-Education Programs and Courses

Growing Up—A Good Time is a nationally recognized course for parents and young people ages eight to fifteen developed by Abby Horak, MS, RN, C, and Laura Pestinger of Emporia, Kansas. In a series of classes, parents and their children share information about sex and sexuality, physical development, communication, decision making, and values. For information, contact Abby Horak at 913-

825-4165 or 913-296-7100 or write the authors at 457 Queens Road, Salina, KS 67401.

For information about various sex-education programs around the country and how they are succeeding, we recommend the book *Adolescents at Risk*, by Joy G. Dryfoos (New York: Oxford University Press, $14.95).

Helpful Hotlines

AIDS hotline: 800-342-AIDS.

Teens TAP (Teaching AIDS Prevention) operates a hotline staffed by teens, for teens. The number is 800-234-TEEN, 4–8 p.m. CST.

STD Hotline: 800-227-8922.

NOTES

Chapter 2: How Teens Feel About Life and Libido

1. George Gallup, Jr., and Robert Bezilla, "Religion Important to Many Teens, Poll Says," *Kansas City Star*, Nov. 23, 1991.
2. Pat Ordovensky, "Student Leaders Call Alcohol, Apathy Top School Problems," *USA Today*, June 25, 1991.
3. "Study Provides a Detailed Look into Teens' Private Worlds," *New York Times*, printed in the *Kansas City Times*, May 23, 1984.

Chapter 6: When Sons or Daughters Are Gay or Lesbian

1. P. Gibson, *Gay Male and Lesbian Youth Suicide: Report of the Secretary's Task Force on Youth Suicide*, U.S. Department of Health and Human Services, 1989.

Chapter 7: When the Issue Is Pregnancy

1. "Surge in Children Living in Poverty Is Cited in Study," *Wall Street Journal*, July 8, 1992.
2. Sonia L. Nazario, "Schools Teach the Virtues of Virginity," *Wall Street Journal*, Feb. 2, 1992.
3. Joy G. Dryfoos, "Prevention of Adolescent Pregnancy," *Adolescents at Risk* (New York: Oxford University Press, 1990), p. 194.
4. The federally sponsored WIC (women, infants, and children) program provides nutritional supplements to qualifying low-income women and their preschool-aged children.

Chapter 8: Sex in a Sexually Unsafe World

1. "Teenagers and AIDS," *Newsweek*, Aug. 3, 1992.